The Science of Writing Characters

The Science of Writing Characters

Using Psychology to Create Compelling Fictional Characters

Kira-Anne Pelican

BLOOMSBURY ACADEMIC

NEW YORK • LONDON • OXFORD • NEW DELHI • SYDNEY

BLOOMSBURY ACADEMIC
Bloomsbury Publishing Inc
1385 Broadway, New York, NY 10018, USA

BLOOMSBURY, BLOOMSBURY ACADEMIC and the Diana logo are trademarks of
Bloomsbury Publishing Plc

First published in the United States of America 2021

Cover design: Namkwon Cho
Cover image © Jose A. Bernat Bacete/Getty Images

Library of Congress Cataloging-in-Publication Data

Names: Pelican, Kira-Anne, author.
Title: The science of writing characters: using psychology to create compelling fictional
characters / Kira-Anne Pelican.
Description: New York : Bloomsbury Academic, 2020. | Includes bibliographical
references and index.
Identifiers: LCCN 2020030088 (print) | LCCN 2020030089 (ebook) |
ISBN 9781501357244 (paperback) | ISBN 9781501357251 (hardback) |
ISBN 9781501357237 (epub) | ISBN 9781501357220 (pdf)
Subjects: LCSH: Fiction–Technique. | Fiction–Psychological aspects. | Characters and
characteristics in literature. | Fictitious characters–Psychological aspects. | Typology
(Psychology) | Creative writing–Authorship. | Motion picture authorship.
Classification: LCC PN3383.C4 P45 2020 (print) | LCC PN3383.C4 (ebook) |
DDC 808.3/97–dc23
LC record available at https://lccn.loc.gov/2020030088
LC ebook record available at https://lccn.loc.gov/2020030089

ISBN: HB: 978-1-5013-5725-1
PB: 978-1-5013-5724-4
ePDF: 978-1-5013-5722-0
eBook: 978-1-5013-5723-7

Typeset by Deanta Global Publishing Services, Chennai, India
Printed and bound in the United States of America

To find out more about our authors and books visit www.bloomsbury.com
and sign up for our newsletters.

To the storytellers whose characters will shake up the status quo and inspire generations to come.
We need you, perhaps more than we ever have.

Contents

Illustrations

Figures

Tables

Acknowledgements

First and foremost, I thank Katie Gallof, my editor at Bloomsbury Academic, for her support in my long journey from proposal to published text. I must also thank the anonymous and not-so-anonymous reviewers whose comments have undoubtedly made this a better book. Special thanks go to Dr Linda Seger for her unwavering encouragement and wise words. My gratitude also extends to Alexandra Leaney, for reviewing an early draft and allowing me to teach a module based on this book at the University of Suffolk. Thanks also to Elliot Grove for creating a space for my Deep Characterisation workshops at Raindance, to Chris Jones for lending me his stage at the London Screenwriters Festival, and to Anna Bielak, for inviting me to present a workshop based on ideas in this book at Warsaw Film School's Script Fiesta. I am also indebted to the many writers who have come along to my talks and workshops, and to my wonderful students. It was your repeated requests for this book that made it happen. Your thoughtful questions made me dig deeper into the research and uncover areas that I'd missed, significantly strengthening this book as a result. My personal thanks also extend to my family for encouraging me at every step along the way – to my parents Alex and Gudrun, to Aasaf, and to Orient, who delights and amazes me every day.

1

Introduction

Behind me, on the shelves in my study, are dozens of books. There are several shelves of my favourite novels, bound and published screenplays, stage plays and collections of short stories. Open their pages and living breathing characters take our hands and pull us into their worlds. We travel with them to new places, form new relationships and encounter new things. We step outside our everyday lives, take different points of view and experience life events that we might never have had otherwise. We're taken on moving emotional journeys that we continue to think about even after we close the last pages of our book and return the volume to our shelves.

Another shelf in my library is dedicated to books on writing. Books which remind us that characters are at the centre of our stories, and that we need to make them rich and complex with interesting emotional lives. Many of these books make other claims too: that characters are transformed by their experiences; that they must start their journeys pursuing external goals, and return home having fulfilled previously unrecognized internal needs. For many years in my work as a writer, researcher and script consultant, I've been wondering about the validity of these claims. Are they culturally propagated, formulaic inventions, or could it be that these narrative patterns reflect fundamental truths about our human nature? If so, is the scientific study of the human mind best placed to answer these questions? Furthermore, given how ill-defined our understanding of what is required to make a character rich, complex and emotionally compelling, is there any more that we can learn from psychology that could help shed light on this process?

It may be that our lack of detailed, procedural knowledge about how to write memorable, compelling and believable characters is best explained by the fact that writing great characters is an intuitive talent that few are born with, but most aren't. Or it may be, as I'm going to argue in this book, that we find it hard to pinpoint what exactly needs to go into creating a great character because we haven't yet been thinking about characters in terms of the right framework, and that this is why when talking about characters, our vocabulary is limited to vague generalities like 'complex', 'rich', 'nuanced', 'engaging', 'thin', 'flat', 'strong' and 'cartoonlike'. This, of course, doesn't mean that if we improve our framework we are handed the right craft skills to make everyone a good writer, but it may help deepen our understanding of the elements required to write a compelling character, and enrich our psychological vocabularies. This book sets out to propose this new framework for writers.

Who is this book for?

This book is for everyone who creates fictional characters and has an interest in using insights from psychological research to create more engaging characters. It is for screenwriters, playwrights and novelists, writers of games, short stories and radio plays. It may also be useful for directors, development consultants, literary consultants and script editors whose work involves analyzing and developing fictional characters. My hope is that this book will span the varied needs of writers just starting out, university students looking for a core text on characterization and professionals wanting to broaden their insights.

This is not to say that I've written a book for all writers. It is evident that some writers have an instinct for the mimetic arts and understand how to capture character. Many prefer to work intuitively, and find that more analytical approaches impinge on their creativity. However, for the majority of writers, the process of developing a character is a craft skill that needs to be honed through years of practice. For these writers, additional knowledge about what is required to create believable and interesting complexity in a character can be immensely useful. If you are one of these writers, you may already be writing characters that are fairly well constructed but missing some as yet intangible quality to make them stand out from the crowd. You may be wondering how you should go about addressing notes on your latest draft that suggest that your characterization needs a bit more work. Or you may already be interested in psychology and looking for a new approach towards character development. Whichever kind of these writers you are, I've written this book for you.

What makes a great character?

Before we go any further and start trying to define what makes a compelling character, we first need to ask if there is any consensus about which characters are great. Given that many of the same characters appear on list after list compiled by critics, or chosen by public vote, the answer appears to be yes. Beginning with film characters, among those most frequently appearing on lists by the American Film Institute, *Empire* magazine, Filmsite and Ranker.com are Indiana Jones (from the franchise beginning with *Raiders of the Lost Ark*, 1981), Ellen Ripley (the *Alien* franchise, 1979–97), James Bond (from the franchise beginning with *Dr No*, 1962), Clarice Starling (*The Silence of the Lambs*, 1991 and *Hannibal*, 2001) and Han Solo (the *Star Wars* franchise, 1977–). From television and streaming content, we can add Tony Soprano (*The Sopranos*, 1999–2007), *Fleabag* (2016–19), Walter White (*Breaking Bad*, 2008–13), Tyrion Lannister (*Game of Thrones*, 2011–19) and Beth Pearson (*This is Us*, 2016–).

Turning to literary fiction, lists of the greatest characters of all time usually include Elizabeth Bennet from *Pride and Prejudice* (Austen, 1813), Becky Sharp from *Vanity Fair* (Thackeray, 1847), Jay Gatsby from *The Great Gatsby* (Fitzgerald, 1925) and Holden Caulfield from *The Catcher in the Rye* (Salinger, 1951). From popular fiction we can add Hermione Granger from the *Harry Potter* series (Rowling, 1997–2007), Katniss Everdeen from *The Hunger Games* (Collins, 2008–) and *Matilda* (Dahl, 1988).

So, what is it that these characters have in common? First and foremost, they are *believable*. We, of course, know that they are textual constructions, but once we are transported into their worlds we invest in them emotionally, we root for them and we may even continue to wonder about their fictional lives after the story has ended. We talk about these characters as though they exist beyond their fictional worlds and are almost real. This is certainly not to say that all fictional characters are believable. Many writers set out to create psychologically credible characters and don't pull it off. Other writers, particularly postmodern authors, set out to challenge the convention that characters are portrayed as believable, consistent and having an identifiable and unique 'self'. Characters in postmodern fiction may have fluid or multiple selves. So rather than being imitations of our selves, these postmodern characters have been described as ciphers or even 'word-beings'.[1] The focus of this book, however, is on the most popular characters that fill our shelves, and these characters are nearly always believable.

One reason why the most popular fictional characters are believable is that we perceive them to be realistically complex. But what does that mean? The British writer E. M. Forster made a start on answering this question when he defined some characters as being *round*, and others *flat*. By his definition, round characters are complex and have the capability of surprising us, while flat characters may be expressed by a single quality or idea.[2] Forster observed that both types of characters have their places in fiction. While having complexity is generally a requisite of the main character in more realistic fictional stories, Forster noted that flatter characters are useful in smaller roles because of their consistency and the fact that they usually don't transform. Because of this they don't distract the reader away from the main storyline.

In Chapter 2 we'll be taking a look at the meaning of complexity or roundness of character from a psychological perspective. Research demonstrates that the complexity of all aspects of our personality is most reliably described and captured across five dimensions, known as the 'Big Five'. Personality psychologists have found that the Big Five dimensions are at the very core of character. They describe who we are, how we are likely to behave, how we interact with other people, and even how we typically feel. The Big Five model describes the 'consistent self' that we experience when we meet someone or a new character for the first time. Since these five dimensions are required to describe personality in full, by definition a rounded character needs to be expressed on all five of these dimensions.

Returning to those lists of great characters, in addition to being complex, believable and consistent, they are also *memorable*. They stay in our minds precisely because they behave in ways that are unlike the average person that we meet. In Chapter 2 we'll be looking at how the Big Five dimensions can be used to create characters who depart from the average and who stay in our thoughts. One essential aspect of their characterization is through their dialogue. In Chapter 3 we'll be investigating how personality influences the way that we speak, from the kinds of subjects that we choose to speak about, the fluency and formality of our sentences, to the choice of words that we use.

In addition to having engaging personalities, memorable characters also tend to be highly *motivated*. They have long-term desires that propel the story forward and drive the plot. And they also have shorter-term motivations that drive their actions from scene to scene and put them into conflict with characters with opposing motivations. In Chapter 4 we'll look at the fifteen universal motivations and why some make characters more compelling than others. In Chapter 5 we will also investigate why protagonists tend to be motivated by desires for status, power and personal freedom in the first half of their journeys, but experience a change of desire towards more connectedness in the second half of their journeys. We'll look at the psychological evidence that suggests that these changes in protagonists' motivations reflect the natural, developmental changes throughout our own lives. We'll explore when we change, why we change and how we change as well as how we can use this knowledge to create more compelling narratives for our characters.

The most memorable characters typically engage the reader the moment they meet them, and then take them along with them on their emotional journeys. In Chapter 6 we'll look at how we can create characters readers and audiences care about and identify with. As we investigate the universal emotions we'll uncover why some are particularly powerful in the way that they move audiences. We'll also explore the six main emotional story arcs and what these have to tell us about their protagonists' journeys. Characters are, of course, rarely alone in our stories, and their relationships with other characters have the potential to be fascinating. In Chapter 7 we'll explore how your characters' personalities should shape the way they interact with other characters, and the twelve different ways in which people try to get what they want. We'll also find out whether opposites really attract and what this tells us about sparking chemistry between your characters. Finally, in Chapter 8, we'll draw all these different threads together in a character workshop. Here you'll be prompted with all the questions that you'll need to answer in order to create a five-dimensional, memorable and engaging protagonist as well as sufficient complexity for the other characters that your story requires.

Is this another book on Jungian archetypes?

No. Although psychoanalytic theory and analytical psychology have been hugely important from a historical perspective in shaping a number of contemporary psychological theories, and provide the inspiration for archetypal character analysis, the mythical school of narrative structure and a popular branch of film theory, these fields are comprehensively covered by other books. My focus in this book is on research and theory from the many other contemporary branches of psychology that are hugely illuminating on subjects including psychological universals, our individual differences, motivations, emotions, and relationships and the way that we change and develop throughout our lives. In the chapters that follow I will be drawing on theories and research from *personality psychology*, *evolutionary psychology*, *neuroscience*, *narrative psychology*, *media psychology* and *developmental psychology*. Before we go on to uncover their research findings that can be most usefully applied by writers, first a few words about each of these branches and their main concerns.

Personality psychology

Central to the framework that we'll be using in this book, personality psychology tells us how personality influences thoughts, feelings, actions, dialogue and motivations in different situations. It aims to show how every individual is different, and which psychological forces cause these differences. By placing personality psychology at the centre of our understanding of the psychological processes behind characterization, we're given a powerful framework with which to understand how to create a fully rounded character as well as why some characters seem 'thin' or 'flat'.

Evolutionary psychology

Taking the view that our minds are genetically adapted to our ancestral environment which existed around 40,000–50,000 years ago, evolutionary psychology examines human behaviour and psychological traits from an evolutionary perspective. Theories of evolutionary psychology usually propose that since there are many adaptive problems to solve, the human brain has evolved as a collection of modular, specialized adaptations, rather than one generalized adaptation.[3] This modular theory explains why we may be motivated by conflicting thoughts, emotions and motivations at any one time – an idea that is central to many fictional stories.

Although evolutionary psychologists point out that our mental structures evolved during the Stone Age, and so are in many ways ill-adapted for the world of today, most scholars believe that our behaviour is the result of interactions between our universal evolved mental adaptations, cultural and environmental influences.[4] This allows us to understand why some story structures, themes or psychological characteristics of fictional characters may have universal appeal and why others just have local appeal. Evolutionary psychology also has the potential to explain why certain attributes of fictional characters are preferred over others, why our relationships with fictional characters are proxies of the relationships that we form in the real world, and why some characters' motivations are more compelling than others.

Neuroscience

Neuroscience is the scientific study of the structure and function of the brain and nervous system. It spans research into the way that individual neurons work, to whole-brain imaging while sensory, motor or cognitive tasks are performed. In relation to creating more compelling fictional characters, neuroscience has the potential to tell us how different characters' actions impact our emotional states, and why our universal predisposition towards optimism appears to be reflected in our stories.

Narrative psychology

Narrative psychologists study the kinds of stories that people typically tell about their lives and how these relate to their identity. From narrative psychology we can learn about the kinds of events that typically shape our lives, and how we believe that these change our identities. Research into narrative psychology reveals the degree to which our lives shape our stories, which, in turn, shape the stories that we tell about our lives.[5]

Media psychology

Media psychology focuses on the interactions between people, media and technology. It explores how we relate to different forms of media and media content and how these affect our psychological processes. Media psychology attempts to answers questions like why we root for certain fictional characters, how we form relationships with fictional characters, and how characters' actions influence our thoughts and feelings.

Developmental psychology

Developmental psychology investigates how and why people change throughout their life course. It tells us about the typical concerns that people face at different stages in their lives as well as their changing motivations. It will be towards developmental psychology that we'll turn when we want to understand whether the changing goals in the typical protagonist's journey reflect the motivational changes that usually happen in our own life course.

How to use this book

Some people like to read textbooks from cover to cover; others prefer to dip into whichever chapter piques their interest. Feel free to work with this book in any way that you please. If you're in a hurry to get through, head to the summaries at the end of each chapter, then peel back and review any areas that you want to understand in more depth. If you're already several drafts into your project, and just want to pick up a few specific tips, then by all means head to the most relevant section. However you choose to work with this book, I hope that it deepens your psychological insights, develops your craft skills and stimulates your imagination. I look forward to discovering your characters!

2

The dimensions of personality

A few months ago, one of my screenwriting clients approached me with her latest project. After working on the idea for nearly a year, she thought she was nearly there. As with all drafts that I'm given, I was excited to start reading. The script began well, bringing to life a fascinating, vivid, and beautifully researched world. Then the main character was introduced and my interest waned. From what I could muster, the story's protagonist was an arrogant aristocrat who needed to learn to listen to others and engage with them in order to become a better leader. Apart from this I learned very little about him. When the protagonist wasn't asserting himself, he was bland. He demonstrated none of the colour or complexities of behaviour that real people have and there was little consistency to his character. While the story's central premise was interesting, and the plotting worked quite well, it was evident that the characterization of the protagonist needed a rethink. Without this, an audience would fail to care about his journey. I sat down with the writer and explained the problem. She considered for a moment then said that she thought she had created a character with a clear external goal, and an opposing need which relates to his flaw. If that wasn't enough to create an engaging and credible character, how should she go about creating one? What is a fully rounded personality, puzzled my writer. And how would she know if she had successfully created one?

In the late 1950s in Arlington, Virginia, military psychologists Raymond E. Christal and Ernest Tupes wrestled over a similar problem. They wanted to understand how the psychological characteristics of another person could be fully described. Faced with the issue of trying to predict which Air Force recruits would perform best in the Officer Candidate School, they hoped they might be able to improve the selection process and speculated that the most capable prospective officers might share psychological characteristics. If this was the case, how should they set about defining what these were? Through a series of experiments the two psychologists found that the personality traits of the prospective pilots consistently fell into five discrete groups, each of which measured a polar spectrum of personality. They named these dimensions as follows: surgency, agreeableness, dependableness, emotional stability and culture.[1] They defined *surgency* as encompassing being talkative, frank, adventurous, social, energetic and cheerful – imagine Tony Stark from the Marvel Cinematic Universe. The next dimension *agreeableness* is best described as being good-natured, emotionally mature, mild, cooperative, trusting, adaptable and kind – think *Annie Hall* in the 1977 film of the same name. The third dimension *dependableness* groups together traits including being responsible, conscientious, orderly and persevering. Bilbo Baggins from *The Hobbit* (Tolkien, 1937) rates highly on this trait. *Emotional stability* measures an individual's predisposition towards being calm and even-tempered. Nearly all action heroes score highly on this dimension. Finally, *culture* is an indicator of the degree to which someone is cultured, independently minded, imaginative and interested in aesthetics – think Ada McGrath from the film *The Piano* (1993).

This model of personality, later renamed the 'Big Five', was subsequently confirmed by a wealth of cross-cultural research.[2] Because of this, a version of this five-factor model remains the standard in social and personality psychology today.[3] Within the contemporary model, the surgency dimension has now been renamed *extroversion* (also spelt 'extraversion'), dependableness has become *conscientiousness* and culture has been renamed *openness to experience*.[4] For writers, this means that to create fully rounded characters, and to understand the way that they think, feel and behave, we need to consider not just one or two dimensions, but all five. As British author E. M. Forster observed, this is not to say that all characters need to be complex and fully rounded, but that your leading characters very likely will, in order to feel lifelike and believable. The five-factor model of personality therefore provides writers with a foundation for understanding what a rounded character encompasses, as well as how to start writing this on the page.

Most writers aren't satisfied with creating rounded and believable characters, they want them to be memorable. So why is it that some characters are more memorable than others, and how does this relate to the Big Five? Because each of the Big Five dimensions is normally distributed across a population, the vast majority of people are moderately extrovert, moderately agreeable, moderately conscientious, score moderately on neuroticism and are moderately open to experience – in other words, they rate somewhere in the middle of the scale across all five dimensions. Since these are the people whom we meet every day, they make less of an impression on us and we are probably better at understanding them. By contrast, people who score towards the extremes of at least one or two of the five dimensions, are more likely to stand out from the crowd. They are memorable precisely because they are *not* versions of the people we meet every day in our lives. We remember them because they are different and because we're often fascinated by those differences and less skilled at understanding how these more extreme people are likely to behave. So, if you want to create a more memorable character, pick at least a couple of dimensions on which your character rates more towards the extremes. These dimensions will become their dominant traits and the ones that we register most quickly when first meeting the character and the traits that we remember.

If we think about the Big Five dimensions as the broad foundations of this approach to creating new characters, then the next stage is to construct nuances and complexities. When psychologists Costa and McCrae realized that not all extroverts are exactly alike - so, for example, some are warm and sociable, while others are highly active and assertive - they proposed that the Big Five dimensions must be further broken down into smaller attributes of personality which they named *facets*. Their experimental studies revealed that each of the Big Five dimensions consists of six facets of personality.[5] In the next sections we'll take a look at what these facets are and how they can be used to create more engaging and complex characters. We'll begin with extroversion since it's one of the most easily identifiable dimensions and one that we most quickly detect when we meet a character for the first time.

Extroversion

Warm, sociable, chatty, full of energy, and high on positive emotions, the comedic protagonist of American TV series *The Marvellous Mrs. Maisel (2017–)* is the typical extrovert. Extroverts are highly dynamic characters who pour their energy out into the world, and feel energized by their social interactions. Often charismatic, extroversion may contribute towards the appeal of a protagonist. Extroverts seize our attention with their loud and assertive voices, their large and free body language, and they compel us to engage with them.[6] Their externally directed energy is often very useful in driving forward a narrative. In the following excerpt from the opening of the pilot episode of *The Marvellous*

Mrs. Maisel, we see the eponymous "Midge" commanding the attention of her audience and announcing herself to the world:

```
The sound of a large room of people rustling in their
seats. A little clinking of forks on china.


                    MIDGE (O.S.)
          Who gives a toast at her own wedding?


FADE IN:


1 INT. BALLROOM - DAY - 1954 1
We come up on the beaming face of MIRIAM "MIDGE" MAISEL.
27, adorable, her eyes sparkle with satisfaction.
Framed by a cloud of tulle, her face is full of perk,
spunk, and complete ignorance that bad things could
ever happen. Because today she has triumphed. Today
is her wedding day.


                    MIDGE

     I mean, who does that? Who stands in the
     middle of a ballroom after drinking three
     glasses of champagne on a completely empty
     stomach, and I mean completely empty
     because fitting into this dress required no
     solid food for three straight weeks. Who
     does that? I do!
```

Source: Excerpt from the 10/12/16 screenplay for the pilot for *The Marvellous Mrs. Maisel* (2017). Written by Amy Sherman-Palladino. Courtesy: Amazon Studios / Dorothy Parker Drank Here Productions / Picrow.

But not all extroverts are alike and in order to better understand their nuances, we first need to look at the six facets of this dimension. As shown in Table 2.1, these are warmth, gregariousness, assertiveness, activity, excitement-seeking, and display of positive emotions.[7] *Warmth* relates to finding other people likeable and wanting to interact with them. *Gregariousness* describes the preference for being around other people and socializing with them. *Assertiveness* groups together qualities including dominance and being forceful. *Activity* tells us about

Table 2.1 The six facets of extroversion

Warmth	Gregariousness	Assertiveness	Activity	Excitement-seeking	Positive emotions

Source: McCrae, R.R. and Costa Jr, P.T., Discriminant validity of NEO–PIR facet scales. *Educational and Psychological Measurement* (1992).

the levels of energy that someone puts into their actions. *Excitement seekers* crave excitement and like to be among the action. Individuals who display *positive emotions* (joy, pride, hope and love) are cheerful and high-spirited.

Character complexity and the creation of interesting characters comes from the combination of scoring high on some facets in any one personality dimension, and lower on others. By way of example, if we compare two fictional spies, James Bond and comedic pastiche Austin Powers, they both rate highly on some aspects of extroversion but clearly have very different personalities. While Austin Powers is warm, gregarious, moderately assertive, active, loves seeking out excitement and shows generally very positive emotions – a combination of traits that perfectly complement his over-the-top, comedic characterization, Bond is active, assertive and a thrill seeker, but less gregarious, generally preferring his own company. He's emotionally neutral, and he's low to moderate on interpersonal warmth. Bond's more subdued displays of warmth, positive emotions and sociability, together with his higher displays of assertiveness, activity and excitement-seeking fit the thriller genre very well. Like Bond, the energy and assertive nature of goal-driven protagonists, who will do everything they can in order to get what they want, is generally essential in driving these high-octane action and adventure narratives.

In fiction, further examples of extrovert characters are everywhere. Among the most memorable examples include Becky Sharp, the cynical social climber in *Vanity Fair* (Thackeray, 1848), *Pippi Longstocking* (Lindgren, 1945), *Indiana Jones* (1981, 1984, 1989, 2008), Basil Fawlty in the British television series *Fawlty Towers* (1975–9), Joey in *Friends* (1994–2004), *Erin Brockovich* (2000), Princess Anna in *Frozen* (2013), Tony Stark in the Marvel Cinematic Universe franchise films, and Saul in *Better Call Saul* (2015–).

Introverted characters appeal to readers and audiences in altogether different ways. Rather than grabbing our attention, compelling us with their energy, and amusing us with their playful banter, introverted characters invite the reader to try and better understand them. Directing their energies inwards, and needing time alone to recharge, introverts tend to be reserved, solitary, serious and slower-paced, which sometimes gives them an air of mystery. Since introverts speak less and tend to keep their thoughts to themselves, novels portraying introvert characters rely on the revelation of personality through actions, observations by other characters, or descriptions of interior thoughts and intentions. Actions and reactions are equally important in revealing characters' internal thoughts in film, in addition to the use of looks, nonverbal gestures or voice-over. In the following excerpt from the Swedish bestselling thriller, *The Girl with the Dragon Tattoo* (Larsson, 2005), the reader learns a little more about the introverted and secretive nature of the titular character Lisbeth Salander through this description from the point of view of her fictional boss:

> She never talked about herself. Colleagues who tried to talk to her seldom got a response and soon gave up. Her attitude encouraged neither trust nor friendship, and she quickly became an outsider wandering the corridors of Milton like a stray cat. She was generally considered a hopeless case.

Source: Excerpt from *The Girl with the Dragon Tattoo* (2011). Written by Stieg Larsson; translated from the Swedish by Reg Keeland. Courtesy: Maclehose Press, Quercus: London.

The mystery at the heart of Larsson's *Millennium* trilogy is reflected in the allure of Salander's character. While she is aloof towards others (low on sociability), naturally submissive (low on assertiveness), prefers her own company (low on gregariousness), and displays neutral emotions (low on positive emotions), she is also moderately active and seeks excitement – facets that are more typical of extroverts. Adding further complexity to her characterization, Salander becomes highly assertive when under extreme pressure. What is essential to making this counter-dispositional (or out-of-character) behaviour believable is that it makes sense given her traumatic backstory. Salander has had to learn to fight in order to survive. While people generally behave in ways that are consistent with their core personality traits, they occasionally act in counter-dispositional ways when they see it as advantageous. When Salander is under threat, it feels very credible that she would believe acting in more assertive and often highly aggressive ways to be advantageous. Third, Salander's assertive behaviour when under extreme pressure is shown consistently. It isn't a character trait that crops up once, and is then forgotten about. Instead, it reads as an essential contradictory part of nature, and for that reason it is fascinating.

Other well-known introverts in fiction show the wide variety of characters that share this dimension. They include Mr Darcy in *Pride and Prejudice* (Austen, 1813), Rick Blaine in *Casablanca* (1942), Will Kane in *High Noon* (1952), Ellen Ripley in the *Alien* films (1979, 1986, 1992, 1997), *Amelie* (2001), Bella Swan the protagonist of the *Twilight* novels (2005–08) and their adaptations to film, Bruce Wayne/*Batman* in the comics and film franchise of the same name, and Little/Chiron/Black in the film *Moonlight* (2016).

How extroverted is your character?

The questions that follow investigate how strongly or weakly your character displays the six facets of extroversion. For each question, consider whether your response is '*Yes, strongly agree*'; '*Yes, moderately agree*'; '*Not sure*'; '*No, moderately disagree*' or '*No, strongly disagree*'.

Warmth

- Is your character generally warm towards other people and do they find it easy to make new friends?
- Or is your character more formal, reserved or aloof with others?

Gregariousness

- Does your character love socializing and think 'the more the merrier'?
- Or is your character more of a loner?

Assertiveness

- Is your character generally assertive?
- Or does your character often feel inferior to others?

Activity

- Is your character full of energy?
- Or is your character inhibited, with lower levels of energy?

Excitement-seeking

- Does your character crave excitement?
- Or does your character prefer the quiet life?

Positive emotions

- Is your character often exuberant and playful?
- Or is your character more serious?

Use your answers to the preceding questions to rate your character on each of the facets of extroversion. How high or low do they score? If they score moderately across every facet, could you heighten or lower the degree to which your character exhibits certain facets in order to make them more memorable? How do these facets fit with your storyline, genre, theme and narrative tone?

Characterizing extroversion vs introversion

Extroversion may be characterized in several ways, which include how a character displays emotion, how they interact with others, how they move, how they look, how they speak and even the kind of activities that they enjoy. These are outlined in Table 2.2. In the next chapter we'll look in more detail at how personality shapes dialogue.

Table 2.2 Emotions and behaviour associated with extroversion versus introversion

	Extrovert	Introvert
Emotions	Positive	Neutral
Movement	Large and free movements	Reserved and defensive gestures
Look	Smiles frequently	Is more serious
	Dresses neatly and stylishly	Dresses more casually
Interactions	Talks to everyone	Prefers close friends and family
	Has good eye contact	Has poor eye contact
	Is playful and makes jokes	Is more serious
	Dominant	Submissive
Dialogue	Talkative and confident	Quieter and lacks confidence
Enjoys	Parties and socializing	Being alone or with close family
	Upbeat vocal music	and friends

Sources: McCrae, R.R. and Costa Jr, P.T., Discriminant validity of NEO–PIR facet scales. *Educational and Psychological Measurement* (1992); Riggio, R.E. and Friedman, H.S., Individual differences and cues to deception. *Journal of Personality and Social Psychology* (1983); Naumann, L.P., Vazire, S., Rentfrow, P.J. and Gosling, S.D., Personality judgements based on physical appearance. *Personality and Social Psychology Bulletin* (2009).

Agreeableness

In one of the earliest scenes in the film adaptation of *The Wizard of Oz* (1939), Dorothy tries her best to get her Aunt Em to listen to what Miss Gulch has done to her beloved pet dog Toto. Although she desperately wants her aunt's support, it's far more important to Dorothy that she doesn't upset Aunt Em by pushing her point. When Aunt Em tells Dorothy to stop worrying and find a place where she won't get into any trouble, Dorothy agrees. And soon she finds that place – in Oz. Like Dorothy, agreeable characters value harmony and getting along with others over asserting their own opinions. They tend to be nurturing, emotionally supportive and altruistic. They are also typically trusting and compliant. Aware of other people's feelings, they do their best to put others at ease and are generally well liked.[8] Characters with these traits are typically likeable, sympathetic and easier for readers to identify with. Other memorable and highly agreeable fictional characters include *Cinderella* (Basile, 1634), *Snow White* (Brothers Grimm, 1812), *Annie Hall* (1977), *Forrest Gump* (1994), Andy Stitzer from *The 40 Year Old Virgin* (2005), and Samwell Tarly from *A Song of Ice and Fire* (Martin, 1996–) and *Game of Thrones* (2011–19).

Diving deeper, there are six facets of agreeableness. As shown in Table 2.3, these are trust, straightforwardness, altruism, compliance, modesty and tender-mindedness. *Trust* is the degree to which someone assumes most other people are well intentioned. *Straightforward* individuals tend to speak the truth and are rarely if ever manipulative. *Altruism* measures the degree to which someone goes out of their way to help others. *Compliance* relates to how cooperative someone is with others. *Modesty* describes the degree to which an individual is unassuming in estimating their abilities or achievements. *Tender-mindedness* is the tendency to be guided by feelings and emotions rather than logic.

While sympathetic and likeable characters are generally more agreeable, some of the strongest characters are highly disagreeable. Valuing their own opinion over the opinions of others, they have little concern for how they may make others feel. Disagreeable characters may also be untrusting, devious, selfish,

Table 2.3 The six facets of agreeableness

Trust	Straightforwardness	Altruism	Compliance	Modesty	Tender-mindedness

Source: McCrae, R.R. and Costa Jr, P.T., Discriminant validity of NEO–PIR facet scales. *Educational and Psychological Measurement* (1992).

competitive and arrogant, which are useful traits in antagonists as we'll examine later when considering how these traits relate to the Dark Triad of personality. But first, by way of example, let's take a look at some of the first words that the disagreeable character of Heathcliff utters, in the opening to *Wuthering Heights* (Bronte, 1847):

> 'Thrushcross Grange is my own, sir', he interrupted, wincing. 'I should not allow any one to inconvenience me, if I could hinder it—walk in!'

> The 'walk in' was uttered with closed teeth, and expressed the sentiment, 'Go to the Deuce': even the gate over which he leant manifested no sympathising movement to the words; and I think that circumstance determined me to accept the invitation: I felt interested in a man who seemed more exaggeratedly reserved than myself.

Source: Excerpt from *Wuthering Heights* (1847). Written by Emily Bronte. Urbana, Illinois: Project Gutenberg.

Disagreeable characters have the potential to make appealing protagonists because they are fascinating. They say the things that social convention tells us not to say, their honesty is often refreshing, and we may find ourselves anticipating in delight the trouble that their blunt words and actions are likely to cause for them. But disagreeable characters can also be sympathetic. Some disagreeable characters win over the reader's sympathy because they are shown to be tender-minded, or have a soft heart. For example, Carl, the obstinate, grumpy and untrusting protagonist of Pixar's family film *Up* (2009) wins over the audience's hearts and minds when his sympathetic backstory is revealed, and he is shown to act on his deep love for his late wife.

Other examples of particularly memorable disagreeable characters include Miss Trunchbull in *Matilda* (Dahl, 1988), Walt Kowalski in *Gran Torino* (2008), Gru in the *Despicable Me* franchise (2010, 2013, 2017), Cersei Lannister in *A Song of Ice and Fire* (Martin, 1996–), Violet Crawley in *Downton Abbey* (2010–15), Riggan Thomson in *Birdman* (2014), *Fleabag* (2016–19) and Logan Roy in *Succession* (2018–).

How agreeable is your character?

The questions that follow investigate how strongly your character displays the six facets of agreeableness. For each question, consider whether your response is '*Yes, strongly agree*'; '*Yes, moderately agree*'; '*Not sure*'; '*No, moderately disagree*' or '*No, strongly disagree*'.

Trust

- Does your character believe in people's intrinsic goodness?
- Or is your character suspicious of strangers?

Straightforwardness

- Is your character straightforward and more likely to be sincere?
- Or does your character use flattery, manipulation and deception in order to get their way?

Altruism

- Does your character go out of their way to help others?
- Or is your character self-centred?

Compliance

- Does your character tend to defer to others?
- Or do they prefer to compete rather than cooperate?

Modesty

- Is your character humble and self-effacing?
- Or is your character considered by others to be arrogant?

Tender-mindedness

- Is your character moved by others' needs?
- Or does your character feel little sympathy towards others?

Use your answers to the preceding questions to rate your character on each of the facets of agreeableness. If they score moderately across every facet, could you heighten or lower the degree to which your character exhibits certain facets in order to make them more memorable? How do these facets fit with your storyline, genre, theme and narrative tone?

Characterizing agreeableness versus disagreeableness

The main ways in which people who are agreeable differ from those who are disagreeable are summarized in Table 2.4 as follows:

Table 2.4 Emotions and behaviour associated with agreeableness versus disagreeableness

	Agreeable	Disagreeable
Emotions	Compassionate and responsive to others' feelings	Indifferent to others' emotions
Movement	Open gestures	Closed and defensive gestures
	May be tactile	Reserved
	Mirrors others' body language	Doesn't mirror body language
Look	Smiling and relaxed	Uncomfortable
Interactions	Cooperative	Uncooperative
	Makes time for friends	Is a self-interested loner
	Submissive	Dominant
Dialogue	Cooperative	Assertive

Sources: McCrae, R.R. and Costa Jr, P.T., Discriminant validity of NEO–PIR facet scales. *Educational and Psychological Measurement* (1992); Naumann, L.P., Vazire, S., Rentfrow, P.J. and Gosling, S.D., 2009. Personality judgements based on physical appearance. *Personality and Social Psychology Bulletin* (2009).

Neuroticism

One of the most memorable emotionally unstable characters to date in early twenty-first-century cinema is Riggan Thomson, protagonist of the multiple Academy Award-winning black comedy *Birdman* (2014). Typical of characters high in neuroticism, Riggan questions his existence, worries about how he is perceived by others and frequently expresses anger, jealousy, guilt and blame. 'I'm nothing. I'm not even here', says Riggan on stage at the climax of his play. He adds later: 'I wasn't even present in my own life, and now I don't have it, and I'm never going to have it.'

Of the six facets of neuroticism shown in Table 2.5, Riggan Thomson rates highly on all. He demonstrates high *anxiety* that often surfaces in the form of his tormenting Birdman alter ego. The tense, jittery energy that accompanies Riggan's anxiety drives the film, sets its tone and even motivates the soundtrack. Riggan also shows high levels of *anger hostility*. He is hot-headed and prone to angry outbursts. Riggan is beset by low moods, a symptom of *depression*. *Self-conscious*, Riggan is preoccupied with how others perceive him – particularly his critics and audiences. He is also highly *impulsive* – he tends to act quickly

Table 2.5 The six facets of neuroticism

Anxiety	Anger hostility	Depression	Self-consciousness	Impulsive	Vulnerable

Source: McCrae, R.R. and Costa Jr, P.T., Discriminant validity of NEO–PIR facet scales. *Educational and Psychological Measurement* (1992).

without much conscious forethought. Last, Riggan is *vulnerable*. He feels unable to cope with life's challenges. Difficult, self-absorbed, angry and disagreeable, Riggan is intriguing rather than sympathetic as a protagonist. He is a character whom we want to understand and learn from. We want to know what he's going to do next, and what is going to happen to him ultimately.

Other memorable fictional characters who score high on neuroticism include the White Rabbit in *Alice's Adventures in Wonderland* (Carroll, 1865), *Anna Karenina* (Tolstoy, 1877), Blanche DuBois in *A Streetcar Named Desire* (Williams, 1947 and film 1951), Bruce Wayne/Batman in the comics and film franchise (1939–), Norma Desmond in *Sunset Boulevard* (1950), Alvy Singer in *Annie Hall* (1977), Richard in *The Secret History* (Tartt, 1992), Princess Elsa in *Frozen* (2013), Kendall Roy in *Succession* (2018–) and *The Joker* (2019).

Since characters who score high on neuroticism are more likely to perceive ordinary situations as threatening, far less dramatic situations are likely to spur them into action compared with the kinds of major inciting incidents that are needed for emotionally stable characters. For Riggan Thomson, his catalyst to action is the falling stage light that injures one of his leading actors. This triggers the chain of events in his mind that places his critical integrity in jeopardy. By contrast, a much greater life-or-death event is required to push emotionally stable action or adventure heroes into motion. For example, in *Skyfall* (2012), James Bond isn't prepared to come out of retirement and return to active duty until the MI6 building explodes and several employees are killed. Emotionally stable characters tend to be calm and far less reactive to stress. They are even-tempered and are less likely to feel disturbed by unusual or potentially threatening situations. Bond is as cool as a cucumber – the typical action hero. Whether in the direct line of explosive gunfire, driving a car off the end of a jetty, or skydiving without a parachute, Bond barely breaks into a sweat. In fact, it is exactly this trait that enables the majority of action heroes to keep pursuing their goals and confronting death-defying situations again and again – they handle stress well.

Related to their emotional stability, action and adventure hero characters tend to be confident and optimistic about their chances of success in achieving their goals. This optimism about their future drives them forward from one challenge to the next. Rather than feeling threatened by the obstacles thrown in their path, they typically view these as everyday challenges that they have the competence to overcome. Emotional stability is an attractive quality[9] – for other characters as well as the reader. We probably enjoy being around calm people because we can rely on their even moods and ability to face obstacles without much anxiety. This appeal of the emotionally stable character may contribute towards the box office success of action and adventure genre films.[10]

Notable emotionally stable characters from fiction include Atticus Finch from *To Kill A Mockingbird* (Lee, 1960), Sherlock Holmes who first appeared in *A Study in Scarlet* (Conan Doyle, 1887), Ethan Hunt from the *Mission: Impossible* film series (1996–), Katniss Everdeen from *The Hunger Games* trilogy (Collins, 2008–10) and film series, Walter White from *Breaking Bad* (2008–13) and Queen Elizabeth II from *The Crown* (2016–).

How high does your character score on neuroticism?

The questions that follow investigate how strongly your character displays the six facets of neuroticism. For each question, consider whether your response is '*Yes, strongly agree*'; '*Yes, moderately agree*'; '*Not sure*'; '*No, moderately disagree*' or '*No, strongly disagree*'.

Anxiety

- Is your character a worrier?
- Or does your character rarely feel anxious or fearful?

Anger hostility

- Does your character often get angry at the way they are treated by others?
- Or is your character easy-going and slow to anger?

Depression

- Does your character often feel lonely or blue? And are they prone to feelings of guilt?
- Or does your character rarely experience these feelings?

Self-consciousness

- Does your character feel uncomfortable and self-conscious around others?
- Or is your character at ease in awkward social situations?

Impulsiveness

- Does your character often succumb to their impulses?
- Or does your character find it easy to resist temptation?

Vulnerability

- When your character is under a lot of stress, do they sometimes feel as if they are going to pieces?
- Or does your character feel capable of handling difficult situations?

Use your answers to the preceding questions to rate your character on each of the facets of neuroticism. How high or low do they score? If they score moderately across every facet, should you rethink the degree to which they exhibit certain facets in order to make them more memorable? How do these facets fit with your storyline, genre, theme and narrative tone?

Characterizing neuroticism versus emotional stability

The main differences between people who score higher on neuroticism when compared with people who score higher on emotional stability are outlined in Table 2.6.

Table 2.6 Emotions and behaviours associated with neuroticism versus emotional stability

	Higher neuroticism	**Emotionally stable**
Emotions	Prone to depression, anger and/or anxiety	Has neutral emotions
	Mood swings	Stable mood
Movement	May fidget	Is calm
Look	Uncomfortable	Relaxed
Interactions	Sensitive and emotionally reactive	Insensitive
	Is argumentative	Not easily upset
		Puts others at ease
Dialogue	More emotional	Calm and unemotional

Sources: McCrae, R.R. and Costa Jr, P.T., Discriminant validity of NEO–PIR facet scales. *Educational and Psychological Measurement* (1992); Mehl, Matthias R., Samuel D. Gosling, and James W. Pennebaker. 'Personality in its natural habitat: Manifestations and implicit folk theories of personality in daily life'. *Journal of Personality and Social Psychology* (2006).

Conscientiousness

Since conscientious characters work hard to achieve their goals, this is an essential personality trait for many fictional protagonists. Whether a story is about a detective solving a mystery, an action heroine trying to save the world, or a young boy trying to find his family, all these narratives rely on the goal-driven nature of their main characters. Take, for example, the central character Andrew Neiman in the American independent drama *Whiplash* (2014), whose dream is to join the Studio Band and become an internationally acclaimed drummer. In the screenplay excerpt that follows, we see that even in the introduction to his character, Neiman's singular ambition is implied. Neiman's eyes are 'zeroed' on his drum stroke; his arms are built from years of drumming; and here he is in the rehearsal room:

```
INT.NASSAU BAND REHEARSAL STUDIO - GEHRING HALL -
NIGHT 1

A cavernous space. Sound-proofed walls. And in the
center, a DRUM SET. Seated at it, in a sweat-marked
white T, eyes zeroed on his single-stroke roll, is
ANDREW NEIMAN.

He's 19, slight, honors-student-skinny -- except for
his arms, which have been built from years and years
of drumming.
```

Source: Excerpt from the final draft screenplay for *Whiplash* (2014). Screenplay by Damian Chazelle. Courtesy: Sony Pictures Classics / Bold Films / Blumhouse Productions / Right of Way Films / Sierra/Affinity.

Former high school chemistry teacher turned meth dealer, Walter White from *Breaking Bad*, (2008–13) is another memorable character, who rates highly on all six factors of conscientiousness that are shown in Table 2.7. First, he is extremely *competent*. Walt's abilities as a chemist enable him to make the purest crystal

Table 2.7 The six facets of conscientiousness

Competence	Order	Dutifulness	Achievement-striving	Self-discipline	Deliberation

Source: McCrae, R.R. and Costa Jr, P.T., Discriminant validity of NEO–PIR facet scales. *Educational and Psychological Measurement* (1992).

meth the market has seen. Second, he rates highly on *order* as demonstrated by his excellent organizational skills in setting up his business and his labs and in the precision with which he cooks. Third, Walt is *dutiful*. His sense of duty to provide for his family contributes towards his move into the drug business. Fourth, Walt is high on *achievement-striving*. Working hard to realize his goals, Walt rises rapidly to the top of the drugs trade. Fifth, Walt is extremely *self-disciplined*: he starts his own meth lab and is involved in every aspect of running it as a business. Sixth, Walt rates highly on *deliberation*, which measures an individual's tendency to think things through before making a decision.

Other memorable fictitious characters who are high on conscientiousness include *Macbeth* (Shakespeare, 1606), *Batman* (1939–), Hermione Granger from *Harry Potter* (Rowling, 1997–2007), Helen from *Bridesmaids* (2011), Claire Underwood and Doug Stamper from the TV series *House of Cards* (2013–19), Andrew Neiman from the drama *Whiplash* (2014), Queen Elizabeth from *The Crown* (2016–), and Valery Legasov and Ulana Khomyuk from the TV miniseries *Chernobyl* (2019).

As we'll examine further in Chapter 5, we usually become more conscientious as we grow older. The most significant growth in conscientiousness occurs in our twenties, during the time when most people need to learn to perform in their jobs and when most people get better at sustaining relationships.[11] This typical growth of conscientiousness in early adulthood is retold in fictional narratives that focus on a character maturing and learning how to better sustain relationships. In the American comedy film, *Ted* (2012), protagonist John Bennett continues to enjoy a juvenile relationship with his talking teddy bear despite now being in his twenties. To his career-driven and competent girlfriend, it is clear that Bennett is going to need to mature in order for their relationship to work. By the end of the film Bennett appears to have found that maturity. He has become more self-disciplined and ordered, and learned to fully engage in his relationship. Although comic, his transformation is credible because it reflects the natural process of development of conscientiousness that most people experience around this point in their lives. In the following screenplay excerpt from the beginning of the film, we meet John in early adulthood, sitting beside his teddy bear:

```
He and John, who sits next to him, are both clearly
stoned as we join them. John, for his part, looks far
too comfortable in the too-worn Red Sox T-shirt he
wears. He eats directly from a box of Fruity Pebbles.
Reaching in for a last handful, he finds the box almost
empty. He raises it to empty the remainder into his
mouth, and accidentally pours Fruity Pebbles all over
```

his face. It doesn't faze him much, though, as he
brushes them off. It's quite obvious that this is a guy
who has never really given up his childhood ... and
has never given up his teddy bear.

Source: Excerpt from unknown draft screenplay for *Ted* (2012). Written by Seth
Macfarlane, Alec Sulkin and Wellesley Wild. Courtesy: Universal Pictures / Media
Rights Capital / Fuzzy Door Productions / Bluegrass Films / Smart Entertainment.

Other well-known fictional characters who are low on conscientiousness include
Oblomov (Goncharov, 1859), Miss Thompson from *Rain* (Maugham, 1921),
Ignatius J. Reilly from *A Confederacy of Dunces* (Toole, 1980), Homer Simpson
from *The Simpsons* (1989–), Dewey Finn from *School of Rock* (2003), Shaun from
Shaun of the Dead (2004), Mo'Nique from *Precious* (2009) and Erlich Bachman
from *Silicon Valley* (2014–19).

How conscientious is your character?

The questions that follow investigate how strongly your character displays the six
facets of conscientiousness. For each question, consider whether your response
is '*Yes, strongly agree*'; '*Yes, moderately agree*'; '*Not sure*'; '*No, moderately disagree*'
or '*No, strongly disagree*'.

Competence

- Does your character feel well prepared for life?
- Or does your character often feel ill-prepared and incompetent?

Order

- Does your character have a clear set of goals and works towards them in an
  orderly fashion?
- Or does your character find it hard to get organized?

Dutifulness

- Is your character reliable and dependable?
- Or is your character unreliable and someone who rarely considers their
  responsibilities?

Achievement-striving

- Does your character have high aspirations and work hard to achieve their goals?
- Or is your character lazy or uninterested in personal success?

Self-discipline

- Does your character try to complete all the tasks given to them?
- Or does your character tend to procrastinate, get distracted, feel discouraged and then quit?

Deliberation

- Does your character tend to think carefully before acting?
- Or is your character more spontaneous and prone to speaking or acting without considering the consequences?

Use your answers to the preceding questions to rate your character on each of the facets of conscientiousness. Once again, consider whether you could make your character more complex, memorable or appealing by making changes to the way that they express themselves across each of these facets.

Characterizing conscientiousness versus unconscientiousness

The main differences between people who score high on conscientiousness compared with people who score low are summarized in Table 2.8.

Table 2.8 Emotions and behaviours associated with conscientiousness versus unconscientiousness

	Conscientious	Unconscientious
Emotions	More positive	More neutral
Look	May dress neatly	
Interactions	Good eye contact	Poor eye contact
	More responsive in conversation	Less responsive and forgetful
	Likely to volunteer for activities	Unlikely to volunteer for activities
Dialogue	Optimistic and polite	Socially uninhibited
Enjoys	Work	Hanging out in restaurants, bars
	Upbeat conventional music	and cafes watching TV
		Social drinking and going to parties

Sources: McCrae, R.R. and Costa Jr, P.T., Discriminant validity of NEO–PIR facet scales. *Educational and Psychological Measurement* (1992); Mehl, Matthias R., Samuel D. Gosling, and James W. Pennebaker. 'Personality in its natural habitat: Manifestations and implicit folk theories of personality in daily life'. *Journal of Personality and Social Psychology* (2006); Watson, David, and Lee Anna Clark. 'On traits and temperament: General and specific factors of emotional experience and their relation to the five-factor model'. *Journal of Personality* (1992); Borkenau, Peter, and Anette Liebler. 'Observable Attributes as Manifestations and Cues of Personality and Intelligence'. *Journal of Personality* (1995); Rentfrow, Peter J., and Samuel D. Gosling. 'The do re mi's of everyday life: the structure and personality correlates of music preferences'. *Journal of Personality and Social Psychology* (2003).

Openness to experience

Of all George R. R. Martin's characters in *A Song of Ice and Fire* (1996–), Tyrion Lannister, the brilliant mischievous dwarf, is his favourite. 'He is the grayest of the gray. In every conventional sense, he is on the wrong side but you have to agree with some of the things he is doing while loathing others. He is very smart and witty, and that makes him fun to write', says Martin. In addition to being highly extrovert, conscientious, somewhat emotionally unstable and mostly agreeable, it is Tyrion's openness to experience that really defines his character. Like Tyrion, people who are high in this dimension are curious about the world and all that it offers. They grasp new ideas quickly, they are interested in both the arts and the sciences, they think about concepts critically and they often challenge mainstream ideas. For Tyrion and others who are high on this dimension, the world is a fascinating and complex place to learn all about and explore. In seeing the world in shades of grey, rather than black and white, Tyrion is given a more flexible way of thinking about life. It is this flexibility that enables him to adapt well to dramatically changing circumstances, think strategically and navigate his way through a variety of possibilities. Like others who are highly open to experience, Tyrion's curiosity about the world extends to his appreciation of travel, his interest in different people and cultures, and his enjoyment of pleasures of the flesh, food and especially drink. Individuals who are high on openness to experience are also generally more creative, aware of their feelings and are likely to feel moved by art or poetry. This sensitivity extends to their emotional life, which tends to be rich and complex. People high in this dimension tolerate ambiguity in their emotional lives quite well.

Of the six facets of openness to experience shown in Table 2.9, Tyrion rates highly on four. He is high in *openness to feelings*. He enjoys meeting new people and embarking on new relationships. Tyrion is also high in *openness to actions*.

Table 2.9 The six facets of openness to experience

Fantasy	Aesthetics	Feelings	Actions	Ideas	Values

Source: McCrae, R.R. and Costa Jr, P.T., Discriminant validity of NEO–PIR facet scales. *Educational and Psychological Measurement* (1992).

He enjoys trying new experiences, travelling to new places and is generally open to new ways of doing things. Tyrion's high ratings for *openness to ideas* are demonstrated by his love of solving problems, his philosophical debates and his intellectual curiosity. In addition, Tyrion is high on *openness to values*. He is broad-minded and interested in the ways that others lead their lives. Since an appreciation of aesthetics isn't important to the storyline of *A Song of Ice and Fire*, it is harder to determine where Tyrion lies on this facet. My best guess is that he rates moderately on *aesthetics*. On the facet of *fantasy*, Tyrion scores low. Rather than being lost in daydreams and a rich imaginative life, Tyrion is grounded, fully absorbed with the present and all the possibilities that real life offers.

Other notable characters who are exceptionally high in openness to experience include Alice from *Alice's Adventures in Wonderland* (Carroll, 1865), Huck Finn from *The Adventures of Huckleberry Finn* (Twain, 1884), Sherlock Holmes, first introduced in *A Study in Scarlet* (Conan Doyle, 1887), *Pippi Longstocking* (Lindgren, 1945), Willy Wonka in *Charlie and the Chocolate Factory* (Dahl, 1964), Walter White from *Breaking Bad* (2008–13), and Frank and Claire Underwood from *House of Cards* (2013–18).

In contrast, people who are closed to experience are generally down-to-earth traditionalists. Taking as an example Bilbo Baggins, the titular character of *The Hobbit* (Tolkien, 1937) and a supporting character in *The Lord of the Rings* novels (1954, 1955, 1956), much of Bilbo's rustic appeal is in his comfortable simplicity. Happy with his lot, he loves the familiarity of home and has absolutely no wish to leave it. When Gandalf proposes to send him on an adventure, Bilbo responds: 'Sorry! I don't want any adventures, thank you. Not today. Good morning!' It is only when Thorin and his band of dwarves hire Bilbo as a burglar in their quest to reclaim their home in the Lonely Mountain that Bilbo's life is turned upside down. Bilbo is the reluctant hero. If it wasn't for these exceptional circumstances, which as the novel suggests awaken his mother's more adventurous side, Bilbo would have lived out the rest of his life in the safety of the Shire. For many of us, Bilbo may be recognizable as the part of ourselves that enjoys everyday simplicity and the comfort of domestic life.

Other well-known fictional characters who are closed to experience include Miss Pross from *A Tale of Two Cities* (Dickens, 1859), Aunt Em from *The Wonderful Wizard of Oz* (Baum, 1900), Roger Thornhill in *North*

By Northwest (1959), Princess Elsa in *Frozen* (2013), Margaery Tyrell in *A Song of Ice and Fire* (Martin, 1991–) and Violet Crawley from *Downton Abbey* (2010–15).

How open to experience is your character?

Fantasy

- Does your character have a vivid imagination and enjoy daydreaming?
- Or is your character firmly grounded in reality and think that daydreaming is a waste of time?

Aesthetics

- Is your character deeply moved by art, music and poetry?
- Or is your character more insensitive and unengaged by the arts?

Feelings

- Does your character place high value on emotional experiences?
- Or does your character experience more blunted emotions and place less value on feelings?

Actions

- Does your character love travelling, trying new activities and experiences?
- Or does your character prefer familiarity and routine?

Ideas

- Is your character open-minded and do they love learning about new things?
- Or does your character have more limited curiosity for the world?

Values

- Is your character willing to re-examine social, political or religious values?
- Or is your character dogmatic, conservative and traditional?

Use your answers to the preceding questions to rate your character on each of the facets of openness to experience. Then examine your answers to ensure that you've created the most interesting and engaging version of the character that you've been developing.

Characterizing openness to experience versus closed to experience

The main differences between people who are open to experience compared with people who are closed to experience are summarized in Table 2.10.

Table 2.10 Emotions and behaviour associated with openness to experience versus closed to experience

	Open to experience	Closed to experience
Emotions	Slightly more positive emotions	
Look	Dresses with a distinctive style	More conformist dress
	Less likely to look healthy and neat	Less relaxed posture
	Relaxed posture	Less expressive
	Expressive	
Interactions	Interested in engaging debate	Has rigid views
	Expresses a wide range of ideas	Is closed-minded
	Likely to have had more relationships	Likely to be married or in a long-term relationship
	Likely to have a more diverse set of liberal-thinking friends	Likely to be politically more conservative
	Politically more liberal	
Dialogue	Loves language and debate	Is more straightforward and simple
Enjoys	Intellectual pursuits, art galleries, restaurants and travel	Prefers familiar and traditional experiences closer to home
	Artistic and intense music	

Sources: McCrae, R.R. and Costa Jr, P.T., Discriminant validity of NEO–PIR facet scales. *Educational and Psychological Measurement* (1992); Steel, Piers, Joseph Schmidt, and Jonas Shultz. 'Refining the relationship between personality and subjective well-being'. *Psychological Bulletin* (2008); Naumann, Laura P., et al. 'Personality judgements based on physical appearance'. *Personality and Social Psychology Bulletin* (2009); Borkenau, Peter, and Anette Liebler. 'Observable Attributes as Manifestations and Cues of Personality and Intelligence'. *Journal of Personality* (1995); Rentfrow, Peter J., and Samuel D. Gosling. 'The do re mi's of everyday life: the structure and personality correlates of music preferences'. *Journal of Personality and Social Psychology* (2003).

The Myers–Briggs Type Indicator

Interestingly, despite the five-factor model being the scientific standard used by social and personality psychologists today, an alternative model – with which many of you may be familiar – still remains hugely popular in mapping employee personalities in the workplace. Based on Carl Jung's theory of psychological types, the *Myers–Briggs Type Indicator* (MBTI) attempts to understand people's behaviour through sixteen personality types, based on the dichotomies of *extroversion/introversion, sensing/intuition, thinking/feeling,* and *perceiving/judging*. Beyond extroversion/introversion, Jung felt that people are best understood through the ways in which they perceive the world and make decisions. He proposed that people who prefer *sensing* the world trust concrete, tangible facts, while people who prefer *intuition* tend to prefer information that may be associated with memories, patterns or hunches. In relation to decision-making, Jung believed that *thinking* types make decisions based on logic, while *feeling* types come to their conclusions based on considering others' feelings, and trying to find harmony. The fourth dimension of the MBTI was later added by educator Katharine Cook Briggs and her daughter Isabel Briggs Myers, who believed that people have a preference for either *judging* or *perceiving* the world depending on whether they act in planned or spontaneous ways. Scientific reviews of the MBTI argue that despite its popularity, it lacks robust empirical support and there are problems with a number of its claims.[12] For writers attempting to build complexity into your characters, understanding them as one of sixteen types is likely to be a limiting process that is more useful for broad brush strokes and stereotypes than creating compelling, nuanced characters.

Personality traits, culture and context

Although individuals' personality traits have been shown to be a very good way of predicting their actions, they are best thought of as *dispositions* towards certain ways of behaving. These dispositions sketch out someone's particular style of doing things, how they usually think and how they usually feel. But as we saw in the example of Lisbeth Salander from Stieg Larsson's *Millennium* series, there are also many occasions in which we act out of character, or in counter-dispositional ways because we believe this to be advantageous in that situation.[13] We adapt our style of doing things according to our social role, cultural conventions, the task at hand, the particular situation we're in and even the time of day. For this reason, most people behave in more conscientious ways when at work. Similarly, introverts often feel compelled to behave in a more extroverted fashion when they feel it is socially necessary.[14] However, acting in a counter-dispositional manner appears to be psychologically taxing, and can only be sustained for relatively short periods of time.[15] When developing a character, think about the times when they are most likely to behave in a counter-dispositional way. Is this in a certain relationship, or under pressure or does a particular environment set them off? Portray this consistency and you'll be well on your way to creating the complexity readers appreciate in their characters.

Personality and gender

Now that we've covered the foundations of personality in the five-factor model, you may be wondering whether there are any other factors that influence our personalities. What about gender, for example? Are there any broad differences between the personalities of men and women? And if so, is this most likely as a result of cultural stereotyping? According to a series of large and well-replicated cross-cultural studies, women tend to be more extroverted, more agreeable, more conscientious and somewhat less emotionally stable than men. Interestingly, and counter-intuitively, these differences are larger in prosperous, healthy, and egalitarian cultures in which women have more opportunities equal to those of men.[16] Whether or not these differences reflect any biological differences, what is vital to remember is that greater variations in personality are found *within* the genders rather than between them. So while on average, women may be somewhat more agreeable, warm, sociable, duty-bound and emotionally unstable than men, female characters who defy these stereotypes are far more likely to stay in our minds. Memorable characters are usually memorable because they are *atypical*.

Personality and mental health

The majority of characters that we've been looking at until this point have been depicted as being in good mental health. But if you're writing a character who struggles with their mental health, you may be wondering how mental health relates to the Big Five. The three most common groups of mental disorders – depressive, anxiety and substance abuse disorders – are linked to high scores on neuroticism[17] and low scores on conscientiousness.[18] Substance abuse disorders are also linked with low agreeableness.[19] While neuroticism is key to understanding the anguish and distress caused by mental health disorders that involve internalizing (including anxiety, depression, PTSD and eating disorders), low agreeableness causes the most suffering for people with externalizing mental health disorders (including psychopathy, antisocial personality disorder and substance use) and for those around them.[20]

The Dark and Light Triads of personality

We have already seen that within the five-factor model, agreeableness is associated with more sympathetic and likeable aspects of personality, while disagreeableness is related to some of the qualities that we generally find more difficult to deal with in our relationships with others. An alternative way of thinking about these attributes is through the lenses of the Light and Dark Triads. These triads group together personality traits that are commonly found in people who are considered to be especially virtuous or antagonistic and so are qualities that are useful to think about as we develop protagonists and antagonists. This does not mean that your protagonists should only have 'Light' qualities and your antagonists only 'Dark', because most people have aspects of attributes from both triads within their personality. More likeable characters, however, tip towards 'the Light', while more difficult and antagonistic characters will weigh heavier on the Dark Triad. Before we go any further, let's investigate the qualities related to both frameworks.

Antagonists and the Dark Triad

Psychologists Delroy Paulhus and Kevin Williams realized that highly antagonistic people who are strongly disliked by others share three personality traits, otherwise known as the Dark Triad.[21] These are Machiavellianism, narcissism and subclinical psychopathy. *Machiavellianism* describes people who strategically deceive and exploit others. *Narcissism* is related to entitled self-importance. Subclinical *psychopathy* describes people who are callous and cynical. All three of these traits are related to disagreeableness. Since the vast majority of villains rate highly on the characteristics of the Dark Triad, a full list of examples would be longer than this book. However, a few well-known favourites include Michael Corleone from *The Godfather* (Puzo, 1969), Darth Vader from

Star Wars (1977–), Jack Torrance from *The Shining* (King, 1977), Claire and Francis Underwood (*House of Cards*, 2013–18), Cersei Lannister and her son Joffrey Baratheon from *A Song of Ice and Fire*, Martin (1996–) and Logan Roy from *Succession* (2018–).

How does your character score on the Dark Triad

Machiavellianism

- Does your character like to use clever manipulation to get their way?
- Or are they always straightforward?
- Does your character make sure that their plans benefit themselves and not others?
- Or do they always consider others?
- Does your character keep track of information that can be used against people later?
- Or would this never occur to your character?

Narcissism

- Does your character consider themself to be special?
- Or do they think they are an average person?
- Does your character love to be the centre of attention?
- Or is this something that they are uncomfortable with?

Psychopathy

- Do others feel that your character is out of control?
- Or do they think your character knows how to manage themself well?
- Does your character enjoy dangerous situations?
- Or do they tend to avoid dangerous situations?
- Does your character enjoy getting revenge?
- Or are they more likely to forgive or move on?

The Light Triad

In contrast with antagonistic characters, people who score highly on the Light Triad tend to see the best in others. They enjoy meaningful relationships and are caring, forgiving, trusting, honest and accepting. These characters aren't quite the mirror opposite of characters who score high on the Dark Triad, but share three qualities of their own. The first of these is *Kantianism*, or valuing others for who they are, rather than as means to an end. The second is *humanism*, or appreciating the dignity of every individual. The third is faith in *humanity*, or believing that we are fundamentally good. Fictional characters who are particularly high on qualities in the Light Triad include Lucy in *The Lion, The Witch and The Wardrobe* (Lewis, 1950), Harry Potter (Rowling, 1997–2007), Russell the boy scout in the animated family adventure film *Up* (2009), Sean Maguire in the drama *Good Will Hunting* (1997) and Samwell Tarly in *A Song of Ice and Fire* (Martin, 1996–).

How does your character score on the Light Triad?

Kantianism

- Does your character enjoy meaningful relationships?
- Or are they always thinking about what they can get from others?

Humanism

- Does your character value honesty over charm?
- Or does your character use deception to get their own way?
- Does your character feel guilty when they've hurt someone?
- Or do they lack remorse?

Faith in humanity

- Does your character tend to see the best in people?
- Or are they suspicious of others and untrusting?

Drawing it all together

In this chapter we've focused on the foundations of characterization. In order to create any new character, we need to know who that character is, how they are likely to behave, think and feel. Extensive psychological research tells us that the five-factor model is the best way of capturing and describing people's individual dispositions towards acting, thinking and feeling in different ways. For writers, therefore, the Big Five dimensions are a powerful framework for understanding what is meant by a fully rounded or complex character, and how individual differences in personality should influence a character's thoughts, emotions and actions. Beyond these Big Five dimensions, further complexity in a character may be captured by the thirty facets of personality. More interesting and memorable characters will make a stronger impression because they rate towards the extremes of some dimensions and facets of personality. They are memorable because they are atypical.

Further complexity may also be added to a character by considering the context of their actions. In your story there will probably be situations in which your character feels most in their element and behaves in their most dispositional ways. At other times, for example, when they are under great pressure, they may be more likely to act in counter-dispositional ways if they believe these to be advantageous.

When it comes to thinking about the degree to which your character is liked or disliked by others – as well as by the reader – the Light and Dark Triads provide an alternative approach that may be useful to consider. Since most people tip towards 'the Light' but have aspects of both triads within their personality, ensuring that your characters have a mixture of Dark and Light attributes means that you are more likely to create believable, complicated and flawed characters rather than cartoon cut-outs.

Now that we've understood the foundations of personality and how the Big Five model can be used to create complex and believable characters, it's time to take a look at how personality and the Big Five dimensions are expressed through dialogue. In the next chapter we'll look at how personality informs not just what your characters say, but the ways in which they say it.

3

How personality shapes dialogue

If I asked you to list ten memorable movie quotes, chances are that among them would be 'Frankly, my dear, I don't give a damn!' Eight muscular words that demonstrate the power of dialogue in capturing the personality, emotions and relationship dynamics of Rhett Butler in *Gone with the Wind* (Mitchell, 1936). It's a novel that I'm including here for the memorable characterization of its two leading roles, despite the film's failure to recognize the heinous slavery that provided the foundations of their world.

Through the content and timing of Rhett's line, we learn that he has finally had enough of Scarlett O' Hara and her ways. Despite his protestation to the contrary, his words are full of emotion. Rhett's words are also a useful reminder that relationships are dynamic and dialogue reflects the current status of this dynamic. His informal phrasing, colloquial language and tough stance reflect the extrovert and disagreeable sides of his personality. The phrases 'Frankly' and 'I don't give a damn' suggest Rhett's age, upbringing and status at the time in which the novel and its adaptation to film were written.

The choice of every word within a character's speech has the potential to be revealing. Psychologists who have analyzed the everyday speech of thousands of people have demonstrated that by listening to someone's voice, we're given cues about their personality, intentions, emotional state, age, education, gender, where they're from and where they live now. In the sections that follow, we'll draw on many of these findings to show how they can help writers create more convincing speech for their characters. However, before we go any further I first need to address the question of whether fictional speech should be psychologically convincing and in at least some way resemble real speech, or whether it is constructed to have an entirely different purpose.

In fiction, dialogue is generally used to serve two purposes – to move along the story and to reveal character. When dialogue simply moves forward the narrative but doesn't feel right for a character, we tend to stop engaging with the story because the characterization sounds expositional and clunky. On the other hand, when we read or hear dialogue that sounds psychologically convincing, we stay engaged with the characters and through this we stay involved with the story. But what do I mean by psychologically convincing dialogue? Should it exactly resemble real-life speech? If you've ever taped an everyday conversation, you'll know that the answer is no. Fictional dialogue distils the 'best bits' of everyday conversation so as to make it interesting, crisp and more efficient. Fictional dialogue is generally more fluent than real-life speech, and well-written dialogue – particularly if it's designed to be performed – tends to have a better rhythm. So why then am I including a chapter based on research into everyday speech? The answer is that fictional dialogue needs to be grounded in the sounds, vocabularies and patter of our everyday spoken language in order to be cognitively convincing. If we have understood that a character is an extrovert, then we instinctively expect their speech to reflect this aspect of their personality. This doesn't mean that an extrovert's speech needs to contain as many disfluencies as we would expect to hear in real life, or that it should conform to all the findings that I'll outline within this chapter, but it does mean that fictional speech should feel right and have the general flavour of the dialogue that we're used to hearing spoken every day.

In order to understand the differences between the ways in which people reveal their personality, status and dynamics of their relationship through dialogue, let's consider the four main aspects of dialogue that disclose character. These are conversational style; linguistic style; content; and vocabulary. A character's *conversational style* tells us about what they are like as a conversational partner. Do they initiate conversation? Are they talkative? Are they a good listener? By contrast, a character's *linguistic style* tells us about the way that someone puts words together to form meaningful, or, occasionally, non-meaningful sentences. These sentences may be longer or shorter, simpler or more elaborate, formal or more colloquial, fluent or disfluent. *Content* refers to the information communicated by a speech. The content of their speech gives us an idea of a character's motivations, beliefs and feelings, as well as the kinds of subjects that interest them. Finally, a character's *vocabulary* reveals certain dimensions of their personality, in addition to their age, education, where they're from, groups they may identify with and the historical period in which they're speaking.

Let's move on now to see how these elements are used by characters who score high or low on particular personality dimensions. If your character scores high or low on a few dimensions, then you'll need to combine elements of all these styles in their dialogue. So, for example, if your character rates high on extroversion and neuroticism, we'd expect their speech to be confident, talkative, informal and emotional.

The chatty extrovert

Instinctively, we all have a pretty good idea of how extroverts speak since extroversion is the easiest personality dimension to detect in dialogue. Extroverts are naturally talkative, charismatic and the first to initiate conversation.[1] They tend to say more, faster, louder and for longer, with very few gaps in the conversation.[2] Naturally at ease with themselves, extroverts love sharing stories, frequently bring themselves into the conversation and are more likely to think aloud and talk just for the pleasure of talking. They're also more likely to complement, and agree with, others.[3]

In terms of their linguistic style, extroverts are typically relaxed and informal in their dialogue. They're much more likely to use positive language, reflecting their emotions.[4] They're also direct. In order to keep up their patter, their sentences are typically shorter, more simply constructed and often aren't even complete. There may be false starts, sentences may be broken off half way through and then repeated or restarted, or they may contain more fillers, including *huh, well, like* and so on.[5] Extroverts also tend to leap from topic to topic in conversation, in a free-flow fashion.[6] It's hard to find a break in the conversation when you're talking to an extrovert.

You can even pick out an extrovert by the kinds of words they most typically use. Reflecting their confidence and assertive nature, extroverts use words like *want, able, need to* more frequently than introverts. They're social creatures, and because of this are more likely to refer to themselves as part of a group. So, you'll hear more *we*'s from an extrovert, than solitary *I*'s. Extroverts are also full of energy and their speech reflects this dynamism. They'll generally use lots of verbs, adverbs and pronouns, which add energy and momentum to their dialogue.[7] Possibly due to their desire to communicate thoughts quickly and keep the conversation going, their spoken vocabulary is less rich than the introvert's and they're more likely to use words incorrectly. That's enough on the theory. Let's take a look at how this works in practice in the screenplay of *Iron Man* (2008), when we first meet the character Tony Stark.

```
2 INT. HUMMER - CONTINUOUS 2

Three Airmen, kids with battle-worn faces. Crammed in
there with them is a Man in an expensive suit, who
looks teleported from Beverly Hills. He is, of course,
```

genius inventor and billionaire, TONY STARK. In his
hand is a drink tumbler of vodka.

                    TONY
          Oh, I get it. You guys aren't
          allowed to talk. Is that it?
          Are you not allowed to talk?

One Airman grins, fidgeting with his orange NY Mets
watch.

                    JIMMY
          No. We're allowed to talk.

                    TONY
          Oh. I see. So it's personal.

                    RAMIREZ
          I think they're intimidated.

                    TONY
          Good God, you're a woman.

The others try to compress laughs.

                    TONY (CONT'D)
          I, honestly, I couldn't have called
          that.
               (after silence)
          I would apologize, but isn't that
          what we're going for here? I saw
          you as a soldier first.

Source: Excerpt from the screenplay of *Iron Man* (2008). Written by Matt
Holloway & Art Marcum and Mark Fergus & Hawk Ostby, with revisions by
Matt Holloway & Art Marcum, Mark Fergus & Hawk Ostby, and John August.
Based on the Marvel Comic. Courtesy: ©2007 MARVEL STUDIOS, INC.

From the moment we meet him, Tony Stark is trying to get our interest. The playful,
relaxed and chatty manner in which he initiates conversation tells us straightaway

that he's an extrovert, and charismatic, too. He's comfortable with himself, he's direct and he's the most assertive and talkative character in the scene. So, it's hardly surprising that he holds the attention of the other characters – and the audience, too. Typical of extroverts, Stark speaks in short, informal sentences using casual language. He's quick to bring his own point of view into the conversation, but also shows that he sees himself as part of this group of people that he's only just met: 'Isn't that what we're going for here?' Extroverts are social beings, who direct energy into their speech and use it to forge rapid social connections.

The quiet introvert

At the other end of this personality dimension are introverts who speak far less and spend much more time listening. They direct their energies inwards, so they also speak more slowly, more quietly and have far shorter conversations than the extrovert.[8] Introverts tend to leave longer pauses in conversation, seemingly to spend more time planning what they're going to say next.[9] Unlike extroverts, introverts tend to stick to just one topic in conversation, which will be something that deeply interests them. They're more likely to bring up problems as well as negative thoughts, and this is reflected in their more downbeat language. As far as they're concerned, when they've said all they want to say on a subject, that's the end of the conversation.

Stylistically, introverts tend to use far more elaborate, fluent and formal language. Their dialogue typically feels more static than the extrovert's, and that's because they use more nouns, adjectives and prepositions. In other words, they talk more about things than actions. Another noticeable difference in their speech is that their vocabulary tends to be richer than the extrovert's and they're also more likely to use words correctly.[10] Let's take a look at the speech of Chiron, otherwise known as Little, in the screenplay from the Academy Award-winning film *Moonlight* (2016). Here's an excerpt from the first scene in which he speaks:

```
INT. JUAN'S HOME - NIGHT

Juan, Teresa, Little gathered at a modest dining table,
the two grown-ups watching the child going to work
on what appears a delicious plate of home-cooking.
```

Something odd about this dining room: the walls are
two colors, in the midst of being painted. A few paint
tins and rollers line the floor, a work in progress.

                    JUAN
          You don't talk much but you damn
          sure can eat. Teresa smiling.

                   TERESA
          That's alright, baby. You talk
          when you ready.

Little looking up from his plate at that, something
about Teresa's voice, her presence, clicking with him.

                   LITTLE
          My name Chiron.
                    (and)
          But people call me Little.

                   TERESA
          I'm gon' call you by your name.

Little shrugs.

                   TERESA
          Where you live, Chiron?

                   LITTLE
          Liberty City.

                   TERESA
          You live with yo' mama?

A nod yes from Little.

                   TERESA
          And what about yo' daddy?

Nothing. Not a blink, not a nod, barely a breath,
just stillness.

```
                    TERESA
     You want us to take you home, then?
                    (and)
     After you finish eating, maybe?


Little lowering his eyes now, gaze going to the table
in front of him:

                    LITTLE
          No.
Teresa and Juan exchanging a look: a confirmation
between them.

                    TERESA
          Okay then. Okay. You ... you can
          stay here tonight. Would you
          like that?


Little nodding yes.
```

Source: Excerpt from the shooting script of *Moonlight* (2016). Written by Barry Jenkins, based on 'In Moonlight Black Boys Look Blue' by Tarell Alvin McCraney. Courtesy: A24 / Pastel / Plan B Entertainment.

Like all highly introverted characters, Little speaks only when he must, and he has been silent in the four scenes that lead up to this excerpt. When Little doesn't want to answer a question, he says nothing at all. It is only now that he meets the warm character of Teresa that Little is shown to feel comfortable enough to open up. For quick reference, Table 3.1 summarizes the main differences in dialogue found between highly extroverted and highly introverted characters.

Thoughtful and agreeable

Highly agreeable people are thoughtful and compassionate – attributes that are reflected in their speech.[11] They're great listeners, try to understand the other person's point of view, generally emphasize the positive and do all they can to reassure their conversational partner that they're on their side. [12,13] They also

Table 3.1 Dialogue differences between extroverts and introverts

	Extrovert	Introvert
Conversational style	Initiates conversation. Speaks loudly, and quickly with few gaps in conversation. More backchannelling when listening (*uh-huh*).	Good listener. Speaks less. Speaks quietly, slowly, tentatively.
Linguistic style	Informal. Sentences are shorter and simpler. Many disfluencies. Uses many verbs, adverbs and pronouns.	Formal. Sentences are longer and more elaborate. More negations and negative emotions expressed. More tentative words. Uses more nouns, adjectives and prepositions.
What do they talk about?	Anything and everything as though thinking out loud, but mostly about social processes, socializing, friends, family, other people, music, religion and sexuality.	One topic which tends to be of personal concern. Often express problems and are more likely to talk about their work.
Vocabulary	Limited and repetitive. Words may be used incorrectly.	Rich. Words are used correctly.

Sources: Scherer, Klaus Rainer. *Personality markers in speech*. Cambridge University Press, (1979); Furnham, A. Language and personality. In H. Giles & W. P. Robinson (Eds.), *Handbook of Language and Social Psychology* (pp. 73–95). Oxford, England: John Wiley & Sons (1990); Pennebaker, James W. and Laura A. King. 'Linguistic styles: Language use as an individual difference.' *Journal of Personality and Social Psychology* (1999); Dewaele, Jean-Marc and Adrian Furnham. 'Extraversion: The unloved variable in applied linguistic research.' *Language Learning* (1999); Gill, Alastair J. and Jon Oberlander. 'Taking care of the linguistic features of extraversion.' In *Proceedings of the Annual Meeting of the Cognitive Science Society* (2002); Mehl, Matthias R., Samuel D. Gosling and James W. Pennebaker. 'Personality in its natural habitat: Manifestations and implicit folk theories of personality in daily life.' *Journal of Personality and social psychology* (2006); Yarkoni, Tal. 'Personality in 100,000 words: A large-scale analysis of personality and word use among bloggers.' *Journal of Research in Personality* (2010).

emphasize their presence in the conversation and as good listeners by using more first-person singulars or *I* words.[14] Perhaps because they're less assertive and often more focused on listening, agreeable people tend to speak in shorter sentences.[15] By way of example, let's take a look at an excerpt from *Annie Hall* (1977). Here's an early scene in which Alvy gets chatting to Annie for the first time after their tennis match:

ALVY
(Still looking over his shoulder)
Uh ... you-you wanna lift?

                    ANNIE
            (Turning and aiming her
            thumb over her shoulder)
    Oh, why-uh ... y-y-you gotta car?

                    ALVY
    No, um ... I was gonna take a cab.

                    ANNIE
                (Laughing)
    Oh, no, I have a car.

                    ALVY
    You have a car?
        (Annie smiles, hands folded
            in front of her)
    So ...
            (Clears his throat)
    I don't understand why ...
    if you have a car, so then-then
    wh-why did you say 'Do you have
    a car?'... like you wanted a lift?

                    ANNIE
    I don't ...
                (Laughing)
    I don't ... Geez, I don't know,
    I've ... I wa- This ... yeah, I
    got this VW out there ...
        (Laughing and gesturing toward the door)
    What a jerk, yeah. Would you like a lift?

                    ALVY
            (Zipping up his bag)
    Sure. W-w-w-which way yuh goin'?

                    ANNIE
    Me? Oh, downtown!

                    ALVY
    Down- I'm-I'm goin' uptown.

ANNIE
(Laughing)
Oh, well, I'm goin' uptown, too.

ALVY
Uh, well, you just said you were
going downtown.

ANNIE
Yeah, well, I'm, but I ...

Source: Excerpt from the shooting script of *Annie Hall* (1977). Written by Woody Allen and Marshall Brickman. Courtesy: Jack Rollins & Charles H. Joffe Productions / Rollin Joffe Productions.

Highly cooperative and altruistic, Annie's main aim is to go along with Alvy in this conversation, rather than asserting her own needs. She even offers to go uptown with him when she actually needs to go downtown.

Interestingly, some disagreeable people, who rate highly on deviousness, try and mimic the way that agreeable people behave in conversation for social advantage. They may pretend to be good listeners, offer complements and agree with others in conversation in order to get something that they want.[16] Let's take a look at how the character Scarlett O'Hara does this in the screenplay for *Gone with the Wind* (1939).

Scarlett and her sisters reach the steps where India
is waiting.

SCARLETT
Why, India Wilkes, what a lovely dress!

SUELLEN
Perfectly lovely, darling!

CARREEN
Just lovely!

SCARLETT
(not looking at the dress, but
looking around for Ashley)
I just can't take my eyes off it.

Source: Excerpt from the final shooting script of *Gone with the Wind* (1939). Written by Sidney Howard, based on the novel by Margaret Mitchell. Courtesy: Selznick International Pictures / Metro-Goldwyn-Mayer (MGM).

Scarlett is, of course, being thoroughly disingenuous here when she complements her rival's dress. Her intention is to keep up the appearance of being warm and socially desirable, while moving away as quickly as possible to find her love interest Ashley. But as screenwriter Sidney Howard indicates, her eyes give her away.

Insensitive and disagreeable

When they're not being devious, disagreeable characters believe in being true to themselves and in order to do this they typically make their point in as clear a fashion as possible. How that makes other people feel is not their concern, so they're far more likely to be rude and angry or to swear.[17] Let's take a look at this in practice in the following transcript from a well-known scene in the American drama *Glengarry Glen Ross* (1992).

BLAKE

The leads are weak? Fucking leads
are weak? You're weak. I've been
in this business fifteen years.

DAVE

What's your name?

BLAKE

Fuck you, that's my name. You
know why, Mister? 'Cause you
drove a Hyundai to get here
tonight, I drove an eighty
thousand dollar BMW. That's my
name. And your name is you're
wanting. And you can't play in
a man's game. You can't close
them. And you go home and tell

```
your wife your troubles. Because
only one thing counts in this
life. Get them to sign on the
line which is dotted. You hear
me, you fucking faggots? A-B-C.
A-always, B-be, C-closing. Always
be closing. Always be closing!
```

Source: Excerpt from transcript of *Glengarry Glen Ross* (1992). Screenplay written by David Mamet. Courtesy: New Line Cinema / Zupnick Cinema Group II / GGR.

Although Mamet has said that he aims to write poetic rather than real dialogue, Blake's speech closely resembles the kind of language we'd expect from a highly disagreeable character. Punchy and direct, Alec Baldwin's character makes his point clearly and in no uncertain terms. He isn't the slightest bit concerned about offending anyone. Instead, he's rude and provocative in order to make sure his point hits home. It isn't just his fellow characters that will remember these lines, we'll remember them as the audience too. The dialogue in this scene is also an excellent example of how fictional speech reflects personality cues from

Table 3.2 Dialogue differences between agreeable and disagreeable people

	Agreeable	Disagreeable
Conversational style	Sympathetic and cooperative. Good listeners, with backchannelling.	Terse, uncooperative and often rude.
Linguistic style	Build personal rapport through the use of first-person singular (lots of *I*, *me* or *my*). Have more positive and fewer negative emotions.	
What do they talk about?	Social processes, friends, family, feelings, home and leisure.	Negative emotions, anger, money/finance, death and why something happened.
Vocabulary		Are more likely to swear.

Sources: Pennebaker, James W. and Laura A. King. 'Linguistic styles: Language use as an individual difference.' *Journal of Personality and Social Psychology* (1999); Mehl, Matthias R., Samuel D. Gosling and James W. Pennebaker. 'Personality in its natural habitat: Manifestations and implicit folk theories of personality in daily life.' *Journal of Personality and Social Psychology* (2006); Mairesse, François, Marilyn A. Walker, Matthias R. Mehl and Roger K. Moore. 'Using linguistic cues for the automatic recognition of personality in conversation and text.' *Journal of Artificial Intelligence Research* (2007); Yarkoni, Tal. 'Personality in 100,000 words: A large-scale analysis of personality and word use among bloggers.' *Journal of Research in Personality* (2010).

everyday dialogue, while improving on it. Using many of the patterns that we would expect from a real extrovert, Blake's dialogue also reveals the way in which playwright David Mamet has tidied these up, and made them more rhythmic. In doing this Mamet captures the essential qualities of personality that are revealed in everyday dialogue while at the same time making these more enjoyable to hear. In summary, Table 3.2 illustrates the main differences between the ways in which highly agreeable and highly disagreeable people speak.

Anxious and emotional

People who score higher on the dimension of neuroticism tend to be more likely to discuss negative emotions, and to use words expressing their sadness or anxiety. Their feelings are also one of the topics that they're most likely to bring up into conversation. As an example, let's take a look at the way that the emotionally unstable central character Riggan speaks in this excerpt from *Birdman or (The Unexpected Virtue of Ignorance)* (2014).

```
                SAM
So. Opening night, tomorrow.


              RIGGAN
Yeah.


                SAM
That's exciting, huh?


              RIGGAN
Yeah. Well ... I don't know.
The previews have been a train
wreck. We haven't been able to
get through a performance without
a raging fire ... or a raging
hard-on. I'm not really sleeping,
you know, at all. And I'm pretty
much broke. Oh, and also, this
play feels like a miniature,
deformed version of myself that
```

```
keeps following me around,
hitting me in the balls with a
tiny hammer.
          (Beat.)
Sorry, what was your question?
```

Source: Excerpt from the shooting script of *Birdman (or The Unexpected Virtue of Ignorance)* (2014). Written by Alejandro G. Iñárritu, Nicolás Giacobone, Alexander Dinelaris, Jr. and Armando Bo. Courtesy: © 2013 DINOSAUR OUT, INC.

It's a great speech and that last line always makes me smile. Carried away by his tirade of negativity, Riggan steers his answer down the rabbit hole and even manages to forget the question – perfectly capturing his neuroticism that is central to this film's narrative.

Cool as a cucumber

In contrast with people who score higher on neuroticism, individuals who are emotionally stable tend to be calm or upbeat in conversation. Outward-focused, rather than inward-looking, they rarely talk about themselves or the way that they're feeling, even in the most stressful situations. Take, for example, the scene from *Alien* (1979) in which Ellen Ripley responds to her first sighting of a cocoon with the body of her colleague Dallas inside.

```
Unexpectedly, his eyes open.
FOCUS ON Ripley.
His voice is a whisper.


                    DALLAS
          Kill me.


                    RIPLEY
          What did it do?


Dallas moves his head slightly.
Ripley turns her light.
```

```
Another cocoon dangles from the ceiling.
But of a different texture.
Smaller and darker, with a harder shell.
Almost exactly like the ovoids in the derelict ship.

                    DALLAS
          That was Brett ...

                    RIPLEY
          I'll get you out of there ...
          We'll get up the autodoc.


A long moment.
It's hopeless.

                    RIPLEY
          What can I do?

                    DALLAS
          Kill me.


Ripley stares at him.
Raises the flamethrower.
Sprays a molten blast.
Another blast.
The entire compartment bursts into flames.
Ripley turns and scrambles back up the ladderway.
```

Rather than going to pieces, in the screenplay the character of Ripley stays cool, calm and collected. A few scenes later, after a narrow escape from the alien and her imploding ship, she is finally able to take a breather:

```
INT. NARCISSUS - LATER

Now re-pressurized.
Ripley is seated in the control chair.
Calm and composed, almost cheerful.
Cat purring in her lap.
She dictates into a recorder.
```

```
                    RIPLEY
        I should reach the frontier in another
        five weeks. With a little luck the
        network will pick me up ... This is
        Ripley, W564502460H, executive officer,
        last survivor of the commercial
        starship Nostromo signing off.
                        (pause)
        Come on cat.


    She switches off the recorder.
    Stares into space.
```

Source: Excerpts from the revised, final shooting script of *Alien* (June, 1978) by Walter Hill and David Giler, based on the screenplay by Dan O'Bannon. Story by Dan O'Bannon and Ronald Shusett. Courtesy: Brandywine Productions / Twentieth Century-Fox Productions.

Ripley's extraordinarily unemotional language is typical of people who rate highly on emotional stability. Interestingly, it is also typical of accounts by recent trauma survivors who typically focus on the facts of their experience in simply structured sentences.

Table 3.3 Dialogue differences between emotionally unstable and stable people

	Emotionally unstable	**Emotionally stable**
Conversational style	Less talkative. More argumentative and speak with more certainty.	Calm, unemotional and more talkative.
What do they talk about?	More likely to talk about themselves and focus on their own negative feelings.	Subjects including friends, sports, money and their physical state.
Vocabulary	Use more concrete words (nouns or events that we can sense). Are more likely to swear.	Use longer words.

Sources: Pennebaker, James W. and Laura A. King. 'Linguistic styles: Language use as an individual difference.' *Journal of Personality and Social Psychology* (1999); Gill, Alastair J. and Jon Oberlander. 'Perception of e-mail personality at zero-acquaintance: Extraversion takes care of itself; neuroticism is a worry.' In *Proceedings of the Annual Meeting of the Cognitive Science Society* (2003); Mehl, Matthias R., Samuel D. Gosling and James W. Pennebaker. 'Personality in its natural habitat: Manifestations and implicit folk theories of personality in daily life.' *Journal of Personality and Social Psychology* (2006); Mairesse, François, Marilyn A. Walker, Matthias R. Mehl and Roger K. Moore. 'Using linguistic cues for the automatic recognition of personality in conversation and text.' *Journal of Artificial Intelligence Research* (2007); Yarkoni, Tal. 'Personality in 100,000 words: A large-scale analysis of personality and word use among bloggers.' *Journal of Research in Personality* (2010).

Table 3.3 summarizes the main differences between the ways in which people who rate high or low on emotional stability speak.

Work-oriented and conscientious

People who are highly conscientious tend to talk a lot about their work, even when they're socializing.[18] In terms of their linguistic style, conscientious people tend to avoid being negative. In comparison with people who show very little conscientiousness, those high on this dimension hardly ever say that they don't want to do something or that they don't like something. They're also less likely to discuss any negative emotions they might be feeling.[19] Instead, conscientious people tend to be quite self-reflective in conversation,[20] for example, when discussing why they made a certain choice.

In the first scene of *The Social Network* (2010), the Mark Zuckerberg character spends what appears to be his first date discussing his best approaches towards getting ahead at Harvard. He's in a potentially romantic situation but all he can talk about is work – he may be hoping that he can make a good impression by mentioning some of his achievements. As is typical of someone who is highly conscientious, Zuckerberg's character uses language that is self-reflective and avoids negativity.

```
FADE IN:

INT. CAMPUS BAR - NIGHT

MARK ZUCKERBERG is a sweet looking 19 year old whose
lack of any physically intimidatling attributes masks
a very complicated and dangerous anger. He has trouble
making eye contact and sometimes it's hard to tell if
he's talking to you or to himself.

ERICA, also 19, is Mark's date. She has a girl-next-
door face that makes her easy to fall for. At this
point in the conversation she already knows that she'd
rather not be there and her politeness is about to be
tested. The scene is stark and simple.
```

                    MARK
How do you distinguish yourself in
a population of people who all got
1600 on their SAT's?

                    ERICA
I didn't know they take SAT's in China.

                    MARK
They don't. I wasn't talking about
China anymore, I was talking about me.

                    ERICA
You got 1600?

                    MARK
Yes. I could sing in an a Capella
group, but I can't sing.

                    ERICA
Does that mean you actually got
nothing wrong?

                    MARK
I can row crew or invent a 25
dollar PC.

                    ERICA
Or you can get into a final club.

                    MARK
Or I can get into a final club.

                    ERICA
You know, from a woman's perspective,
sometimes not singing in an a Capella
group is a good thing?

                    MARK
This is serious.

Source: Excerpt from the final draft screenplay of *The Social Network* (2010). Written by Aaron Sorkin, based on the book *The Accidental Billionaires* by Ben Mezrich. Courtesy: Columbia Pictures / Relativity Media / Scott Rudin Productions / Michael de Luca Productions / Trigger Street Productions.

Easy-going

People who lack conscientiousness are far more likely to speak in a socially uninhibited way. That means they're more likely to swear, speak loudly[21] and express negative emotions[22] than highly conscientious people.[23] In the following scene from the adult comedy *Ted* (2012), the main character John kicks back on the sofa with his talking teddy bear.

                         TED
        All I'm sayin' is Boston women are,
        on the whole, a paler, uglier sort
        than women from the elsewheres
        of life.

                         JOHN
        That's bullshit, what about Lori?
        She's hot.

                         TED
        Lori's from Pennsylvania, not a
        Boston girl.

                         JOHN
        They're not that bad.

John takes a hit from the bong over Ted's next line.

                         TED
        The fact that you have to say
        they're not that bad means that
        they are that bad. They turn into
        drunk, half-white, half-

```
                pink monsters after 2 hours at any beach.
                Ted takes a hit from the bong.

                        TED (CONT'D)
                        (COUGHS)
                Jesus, this is weak. It's not even
                gettin' me high. I gotta have a
                talk with my weed guy.


                        JOHN
                I-- It's workin' for me.


                        TED
                I think it sucks, I'm gonna have a
                talk with him.
```

Source: Excerpt from an unspecified draft of the screenplay for *Ted* (2012). Written by Seth Macfarlane, Alec Sulkin & Wellesley Wild. Courtesy Universal Pictures / Media Rights Capital / Fuzzy Door Productions / Bluegrass Films / Smart Entertainment.

There's no way that characters like John and Ted are going to spend their free time discussing work. For them, there's far more fun to be had talking about girls and parties. As we'd expect from unconscientious characters, their language is casual, colloquial and socially uninhibited. It's also sweary, rude and playful. Table 3.4 summarizes the main differences in the dialogue between people who are highly conscientious and those who are low on this dimension.

Open to experience, loves debate

People who are open to experience tend to love language. They're in their element debating ideas, discussing various aspects of culture, and different values and beliefs about the world. People who are highly open to experience are most likely to be open-minded about the attitudes of others, as well as more tentative about their own. In conversation, they express this through the use of more tentative words, for example *perhaps* and *maybe*. They tend to use longer words in conversation and words that suggest they have insight (e.g. *I realize* and *I understand*).[24] They also tend to express their imaginative ideas. As an example,

Table 3.4 Dialogue differences between conscientious and unconscientious people

	Conscientious	Unconscientious
Conversational style	Optimistic, self-reflective, and polite.	Socially uninhibited. More likely to swear, express negative emotions and speak loudly.
Linguistic style	Use fewer pronouns as well as more words related to communication (e.g. *talk* and *share*). More likely to say *I mean* or *you know*.	
What do they talk about?	Work. More likely to mention their achievements.	Music, people, things that they have heard, negative emotions, why something happened, death and other subjects.
Vocabulary	Use longer words.	Use shorter words.

Sources: Pennebaker, James W. and Laura A. King. 'Linguistic styles: Language use as an individual difference.' *Journal of Personality and Social Psychology* (1999); Mehl, Matthias R., Samuel D. Gosling and James W. Pennebaker. 'Personality in its natural habitat: Manifestations and implicit folk theories of personality in daily life.' *Journal of Personality and Social Psychology* (2006); Mairesse, François, Marilyn A. Walker, Matthias R. Mehl and Roger K. Moore. 'Using linguistic cues for the automatic recognition of personality in conversation and text.' *Journal of Artificial Intelligence Research* (2007); Yarkoni, Tal. 'Personality in 100,000 words: A large-scale analysis of personality and word use among bloggers.' *Journal of Research in Personality* (2010); Laserna, Charlyn M., Yi-Tai Seih and James W. Pennebaker. 'Um . . . who like says you know: Filler word use as a function of age, gender, and personality.' *Journal of Language and Social Psychology* (2014).

let's take a look at the May Ball scene from *The Theory of Everything* (2015) in which Stephen Hawking's character gets to know Jane, his future wife.

STEPHEN (CONT'D)
So--The 1920s. A good time for
poetry, was it?

JANE
'Seek then/ No learning/ from
Starry Men!/ Who follow with Optic
Glass/ The Whirling Ways of Stars
that Pass.'

STEPHEN
Ouch.

JANE
Was it —

They move off across the NEARBY DANCE-FLOOR, and
PASS the JAZZ BAND en route to the LIGHTED FOOT-
BRIDGE spanning a river under which LIGHTED PUNTS
drift by.

                    JANE (CONT'D)
          - was it a good time for science?

                    STEPHEN
          A smashing time actually. Spacetime
          was born.

                    JANE
          Spacetime...

                    STEPHEN
          Space and Time finally got together. People
          always thought they were too dissimilar,
          couldn't possibly work out. But then along
          comes Einstein, the ultimate matchmaker, and
          decided that space and time, not only had a
          future, but had been married all along.

                    JANE
          The perfect couple!

Source: Excerpt from the (November 2013) shooting script for *The Theory of Everything* (2014). Screenplay by Anthony McCarten. Courtesy: Working Title Films / Dentsy Motion Pictures / Fuji Television Network.

In his use of language in this scene, the character of Stephen Hawking demonstrates his love of big, imaginative ideas, typical of people who are highly open to experience. Hawking's character is presented as being articulate, clearly expressing his ideas and using rich, vivid and fairly complex language.

Down to earth, closed to experience

People who are closed to experience prefer the familiarity and routines of everyday life. Because of this, they enjoy talking about their everyday life and occupations.[25] Possibly reflecting their nostalgia for the bygone days, people who are closed to experience are also more likely to speak in the past tense.[26] In the following scene from the British TV series *The Crown* (2016–), the character of Queen Elizabeth II exemplifies this beautifully as she confides in her dear friend Porchey.

> ELIZABETH
> (looks around at the beautiful
> solitariness and the silence)
> People used to laugh at my
> grandfather. He would retreat to a
> gamekeeper's cottage for days on
> end with his stamp albums and do
> nothing all day long except shuffle
> and stick in his stamps. They were
> his best friends. Little scraps of
> paper from all around the world,
> bearing the heads of other lonely
> monarchs. And Queen Victoria used
> to vanish into these forests for
> months at a time.

ELIZABETH tails off. She motions to a plain, stumpy, estate manager's cottage, now visible in the background. Not very pretty, and rather humble. Cut off from the world.

> ELIZABETH
> I'm sure each of us has a single
> image or dream that defines us.
> Who we are. What we want. What we
> dream of. That's mine. A sensible
> sized house. Miles from anywhere,
> no round-the-clock duty. No armies
> of staff. Just me, living in that
> cottage, a simple countrywoman.
> It's the life ...

Source: Excerpt from the screenplay for Episode 210, Mystery Man, Season Two of *The Crown*. Screenplay by Peter Morgan. Courtesy: Left Bank Pictures / Sony Pictures Television Production UK.

Table 3.5 Dialogue differences between people open to experience and closed to experience

	Open to experience	Closed to experience
Conversational style	Love language and debate. More use of backchannels when listening.	More straightforward and simple.
Linguistic style	Often use more tentative language (e.g. *perhaps* and *maybe*). Avoid first-person singular (I).	Are more likely to speak in past tense, and use third person pronouns (*he, she, they*).
What do they talk about?	Big ideas, culture. Better at detecting deception.	Everyday routines and their occupation.
Vocabulary	Use longer words.	Use shorter words.

Sources: Pennebaker, James W. and Laura A. King. 'Linguistic styles: Language use as an individual difference.' *Journal of Personality and Social Psychology* (1999); Dewaele, Jean-Marc and Adrian Furnham. 'Extraversion: The unloved variable in applied linguistic research.' *Language Learning* (1999); Mehl, Matthias R., Samuel D. Gosling, and James W. Pennebaker. 'Personality in its natural habitat: Manifestations and implicit folk theories of personality in daily life.' *Journal of Personality and Social Psychology* (2006).

In addition to the fact that Peter Morgan's characterization of Elizabeth has her telling Porchey that she would prefer the everyday routines of a simpler life, her conversational style is also very much in keeping with someone who is more closed to experience. She initially reflects on her grandfather's life using the past tense and then, using simple language, she tells us about the life she'd like to lead now. Pulling together our discoveries about the differences between the ways in which people who are highly open to experience speak compared with people who rate low on this dimension, I have summarized the main findings in Table 3.5.

Gender and language

The question of whether men and women use language in different ways when they speak remains a hugely controversial subject. Is there any truth to the widely held view that women are better at talking about feelings? And do men really prefer to talk about sports and cars? One of the largest studies to investigate gender differences in language use found that the number of statistically significant differences that exist between the ways that men and women speak is in practice very small. So, while men were found to refer slightly more often to objects and impersonal topics, and women to psychological and social processes including their home, family and friends, in practice the differences mean a couple of words more or less when speaking non-stop for ten minutes.[27] When it comes to writing dialogue in fiction, these differences are negligible. Equally important to note is that studies investigating gender differences in language use have found that variation among the ways that women speak, and among the ways that men speak is considerable. So, my advice again is that if you want to create memorable characters, think about how these characters' speech differs from stereotypes that we may hold and challenges our expectations in surprising and interesting ways.

Language and power

Power dynamics are intrinsic to the majority of our relationships. We don't always know why we think someone has the most power in the room, but we almost certainly know who has it. Some of these cues are nonverbal, for example, related to the distance someone stands from others, but many are verbal. People with more power tend to say *we*, *us* and *our* more frequently than *I*, *me* and *my*. They put the power of group-thinking behind them. By comparison, people with the least power tend to say *I*, *me*, *my* more than *we*, *us* and *our*. People of higher status also tend to interrupt more frequently and speak more loudly than people of lower status. Let's investigate this in a scene from *The Godfather* (1972).

```
INT DAY: CARLO'S LIVING ROOM (1955)

The door opens, and the grim party enters.

                MICHAEL
        You fingered Sonny for the Barzini
        people. That little farce you played
        out with my sister. Did Barzini kid
        you that would fool a Corleone?

                CARLO
                (dignity)
        I swear I'm innocent. I swear
        on the head of my children, I'm
```

innocent. Mike, don't do this to
me, please Mike, don't do this
to me!

                MICHAEL
              (quietly)
Barzini is dead. So is Philip
Tattaglia, so are Strachi, Cuneo
and Moe Greene...I want to square
all the family accounts tonight.
So, don't tell me you're innocent;
admit what you did.

CARLO is silent; he wants to talk but is terrified.

                MICHAEL
            (almost kindly)
Don't be frightened. Do you think
I'd make my sister a widow? Do
you think I'd make your children
fatherless? After all, I'm
Godfather to your son. No, your
punishment is that you're out of
the family business. I'm putting
you on a plane to Vegas--and I want
you to stay there. I'll send Connie
an allowance, that's all. But don't
keep saying you're innocent; it
insults my intelligence and makes
me angry.

Source: Excerpt from the third draft screenplay for *The Godfather* (1972). Written by Mario Puzo and Francis Ford Coppola. Based on the novel by Mario Puzo. Courtesy: Paramount Pictures.

It's evident from this scene that Michael has the power and Carlo knows it. When Michael accuses Carlo of fingering Sonny, his repeated use of the word *you* emphasizes his superior status. Imploring Michael to believe that he is innocent, Carlo persistently uses the personal pronouns *I* and *me*. Towards the

Table 3.6 Dialogue differences between people who have higher and lower status

	High status	Low status
Conversational style	Tend to interrupt more often. Tend to speak more loudly.	Rarely interrupt. Typically speak more quietly.
Linguistic style	Tend to say *we, us, our* (first-person plural pronouns) more than *I, me, my*. Tend to say *you* or *your* more often.	Tend to say *I, me, my* (first-person singular pronouns) more than *we, us, our*.

Sources: Pennebaker, James W. *The Secret Life of Pronouns: What Our Words Say About Us.* New York: Bloomsbury Press (2011); Hall, Judith A., Erik J. Coats and Lavonia Smith LeBeau. 'Nonverbal behaviour and the vertical dimension of social relations: a meta-analysis.' *Psychological Bulletin* (2005).

end of this scene, Michael relents a little and his use of more *I*'s goes some way towards redressing the power balance (see Table 3.6).

The language of intimacy

In the romantic comedy film *When Harry Met Sally* (1989), screenwriter Nora Ephron demonstrates how dialogue has the ability to reveal intimate connections between characters, as well the lack of connection. In the excerpt that follows, where Harry first meets Sally, his future romantic partner, it's evident from their first few lines of dialogue that they have no real interest in each other. They aren't listening to each other; their thoughts are elsewhere and they sound out of sync.

> SALLY
>
> I have this all figured out. It's
> an 18 hour trip, which breaks down
> to 6 shifts of 3 hours each. Or,
> alternatively, we could break it
> down by mileage. There's a map
> on the visor, I've marked it to
> show the locations where we change
> shifts. You can do three hours?
>
> HARRY
> (offering her one)
> Grape?

                              SALLY
            No. I don't like to eat between meals.

Source: Excerpt from 8/23/88 (pink) revision screenplay for *When Harry Met Sally* (1989). Written by Nora Ephron, Rob Reiner and Andrew Scheinman. Copyright © Castle Rock Ent.

By the end of the film Sally's relationship with Harry has entirely changed. They're in love, and their now intimate connection is reflected in their dialogue. Throughout the scene that follows, the couple listen intently to each other. They echo and repeat each other's words and phrases. To the audience it is clear that they are perfectly in sync.

                         HARRY (V.O.)
            The first time we met we hated each
            other.

                         SALLY(V.O.)
            You didn't hate me, I hated you.
                            (beat)
            The second time we met he didn't
            even remember me.

                         HARRY (V.O.)
            I did too. I remembered you.
                          (a long beat)
            The third time we met we became
            friends.

                         SALLY (V.O.)
            We were friends for a long time.

                         HARRY (V.O.)
            And then we weren't.

                         SALLY (V.O.)
            And then we fell in love.

Source: Excerpt from 8/23/88 (pink) revision screenplay for *When Harry Met Sally* (1989). Written by Nora Ephron, Rob Reiner and Andrew Scheinman. Copyright © Castle Rock Ent.

Age, social class, communities and dialects

Other factors to consider when writing dialogue are the ages of the characters that you're writing, where they live now, where else they've lived, their social class and the specific groups or communities they belong to. As people grow older, they tend to be more positive in their conversations, using more words relating to good feelings and less relating to negative feelings. They also talk less about themselves, speak more about the future, talk less about the past, and voice more complex ideas.[28] Where people live and where they're from also affects the way that they speak. Regional dialects can often be spotted by listeners within just a few seconds, and these include differences in the way that different groups use grammar, phrases and colloquialisms, as well as the way in which some things are named. The way that we speak also provides insights into our social class, which is related to our education and socio-economic status. In practice, these differences are small, but psychologists have found that in the United States – and possibly across all English-speaking countries – people from higher social classes typically use longer words and talk more about things, while people from lower social classes use shorter words and slightly more present tense verbs.[29]

Context

Whenever we're thinking about how someone is likely to behave in a situation, considering the context is key and the same is true when we're thinking about dialogue. We change the way that we speak, and what we speak about according to who we speak to, the present dynamics of that relationship and where it is that our conversation is taking place. While at work in an office, people tend to use more *we* words, more complex language and express more negative feelings. When talking about sports, people tend to use more upbeat language, fewer *I* words and less introspection. When talking over a sit down meal, people tend to tell more stories, use more *I* and *s/he* words and speak in the past tense. By comparison, when walking and talking, people tend to use more personal, superficial and upbeat language, typically in the present tense.[30] There are also typically different subjects that we prefer to discuss in different relationships. We may have a Friday night with a pub friend with whom we joke around and talk politics, a lunch colleague with whom we share office gossip and politics, and a close friend from our schooldays with whom we discuss more personal concerns and relationships over a quiet dinner. There is a lot to think about here, but your reader knows when you get it right.

Drawing it all together

If you were going to take away just one point from this chapter it should be that everyone's dialogue is unique and that our personalities are reflected not just in what we say, but when we choose to say it, who we say it to, and how we say it. Although extroversion is the easiest personality dimension to detect within speech, we also instinctively know whether a character is agreeable, emotionally stable and, with a little more thought, conscientious and open to experience. Dialogue reveals how close a character is to another in a relationship, their status compared to their conversational partner, their shared interests, as well as ideas that they don't share. Dialogue also provides cues suggesting a character's age, education and background. Since we are highly attuned to the patterns of natural speech and the important cues that these reveal, fictional dialogue is mostly likely to hold an audience's attention when it sounds convincing. This doesn't mean that direct dialogue within fiction should precisely mimic everyday speech, but that writers can improve their chances of keeping their audiences engaged with their characters if they understand and implement at least some of the most essential features of dialogue that I've outlined in this chapter.

Having spent the last two chapters investigating how personality shapes our actions, reactions, thoughts, feelings and dialogue, in the next chapter we'll go on to look at motivations, and how these spur your hopefully now-well-constructed character into action.

4

Motivating character

Motivations are the forces that we call upon to bring our characters to life. Goals initiate our behaviour, focus our attention and draw us into conflict with others. They bring energy, forward momentum and a sense of direction to our stories. Through a protagonist's goal we form hopes and fears about whether they will achieve it, and through these hopes and fears we understand where a story is going. It is in this gap between our greatest hopes for a character, and our worst fears for them, that tension is created. The greater the gap, the greater the tension. Motivations have shaped our stories since the very first tales were told. Along with environmental and cultural influences, our goals reflect our ancient ancestral struggles to protect ourselves, find a partner, care for our families, form friendships and alliances and perhaps also to create a meaningful life. It is because these goals are universal that well-constructed stories with engaging characters have the potential to travel the world. But what are these universal goals and why do we act on some motivations with more urgency than others? In the sections that follow we'll take a closer look at the fifteen universal motivations and why stories about some of these are more likely to seize our attention.

We'll also investigate why a protagonist's conflicting motivations are at the heart of so many stories. Could these central conflicts mirror the internal conflict that we typically experience in our own lives? Related to this, we'll uncover why the motivations of central characters usually transform, and why this generally reflects the same pattern of change. Screenwriting manuals often suggest that characters must start their journeys motivated by a conscious and explicit external goal, but complete their journeys motivated by an unconscious or subconscious internal need. From a psychological perspective, what does this actually mean? And is there anything that we can learn from the ways in which our motivations usually change as we grow older that could help us better understand why and how character motivations typically change across the course of the narrative? In the sections that follow, we'll take a look at the psychological theories and research that tell us more about these ideas and why a character's motivations are an essential element in their characterization.

The fifteen evolutionary motivations

For many years, psychologists have been fascinated by what motivates us. Numerous competing theories of motivations have been developed, but the vast majority of these fail to explain *why* we have motivations and the purpose that they serve. This changed when evolutionary psychologists, including Larry Bernard and his team, theorized that our motivations must have evolved during our ancestral environment as adaptations that would increase our chances of not only our own reproduction and survival, but also the survival of our closest family[1]. Bernard and his colleagues propose that all motivations fall into five groups, according to who they impact. Motivations relating to *survival* directly help the individual. Motivations relating to *finding a partner and having children* act at the interpersonal level, between two people. Motivations that involve *family love* promote survival of the family. *Forming friendships and alliances* involves larger non-family groups. Finally, motivations relating to *creating a legacy and a meaningful life* have the potential to act across society. Let's take a closer look at each of these in turn.

Survival

Motivations related to promoting survival are believed to have arisen early in our development as humans. They act on the nonconscious, *instinctive* part of our brain in which our raw emotions and motivations appear to be closely linked. This means that we respond rapidly and instinctively to threats to our survival. It may also mean that we're primed to listen more closely to stories about characters whose survival is threatened, in order for us to learn more about these situations should we encounter them.[2]

In order to survive we need to stay *safe*, which means protecting ourselves, our possessions and our territory from antagonistic forces. We also need to stay *healthy*. There are times when we need to be *aggressive* in order to protect ourselves, assert our dominance and gain power. *Curiosity* is also important because it involves learning to better understand our environment, its dangers, challenges and opportunities. The final motivation within this domain is *play*,

Table 4.1 Evolutionary motivations relating to survival

Motivation	Film	Protagonist
Safety	*It* (2017)	Bill Denbrough
	Jurassic World (2015)	Owen Grady
	Independence Day (1996)	David Levinson
Health	*Bird Box* (2018)	Malorie Hayes
	28 Days Later (2002)	Jim
	Safe (1995)	Carol White
Aggression	*A History of Violence (2005)*	Tom Stall
	Kill Bill: Volume 1 (2003)	The Bride
	La Haine (1995)	Vinz, Hubert and Saïd
Curiosity	*Alice in Wonderland* (2010)	Alice
	Willy Wonka and the Chocolate Factory (1971)	Charlie Bucket
Play	*Ready Player One* (2018)	Wade Watts
	The Game (1997)	Nicholas Van Orton
	Jumanji (1995)	Alan and Sarah

which helps us learn about social rules by testing them in mock aggressive situations.[3] Enough with the theory. In Table 4.1 we take a look at how these survival motivations are used to drive the main characters of a number of well-known films.

Finding a partner

You won't need a psychologist to tell you that finding the right partner is another of our strongest motivations. In addition to our instinctive desire to have *sex*, other motivations within this domain are thought to have evolved in order to improve our chances of attracting a mate via communicating or improving our status. These status-related motivations act in four key areas: through improving or showing off our *physical skills*, our *mental skills*, our *appearance* and our *wealth*.[4] This isn't to say that when we're competing in sports, taking creative writing classes or polishing off our novels, we're consciously thinking about finding a new (or better) partner, but that these are likely the reasons why these status-related motivations originally evolved. Since we have conscious control over our status-related desires, their expression is shaped by the culture and society that we live within. For some, the driver of a red Ferrari may be as enchanting as a peacock's display to a peahen, but for others the equivalent may be the writer of an insightful political Tweet.

Table 4.2 illustrates how these dating and status-related motivations drive the protagonists of some well-known films.

Table 4.2 Evolutionary motivations relating to finding a partner and having children

Motivation	Film	Protagonist
Dating/sex	*Carol* (2015)	Carol
	The 40-Year-Old Virgin (2005)	Andy Stitzer
	Brokeback Mountain (2005)	Jack Twist & Ennis Del Mar
	Gone with the Wind (1939)	Scarlett O'Hara
Displaying/improving physical skills	*I, Tonya* (2017)	Tonya Harding
	Chariots of Fire (1981)	Harold Abrahams
	Rocky (1976)	Rocky
Displaying/improving mental skills	*The Theory of Everything* (2014)	Stephen Hawking
	The Social Network (2010)	Mark Zuckerberg
	Amadeus (1984)	Antonio Salieri
Displaying/improving appearance	*I Feel Pretty* (2018)	Renee Bennet
	Big (1988)	Josh Baskin
	Cover Girl (1944)	Rusty
Demonstrating/ acquiring wealth	*The Wolf of Wall Street* (2013)	Jordan Belfort
	Glengarry Glen Ross (1983)	Shelley Levene
	Gentlemen Prefer Blondes (1953)	Lorelei Lee

(Family) love

Once partners have found each other, it's thought that love and *affection* must have evolved to foster a cooperative relationship and tend for any children in order to keep the partnership and the family group together.[5] Table 4.3 illustrates how affection motivates the protagonists of some well-known films.

Table 4.3 Evolutionary motivations relating to love

Motivation	Film	Protagonist
Affection	*Amour* (2012)	Georges
	Finding Nemo (2003)	Marlin
	Mrs Doubtfire (1993)	Daniel Hillard

Forming friendships and alliances

Another group of motivations help us to form better friendships and work in groups with others. The desire to form these friendships and alliances would very likely have evolved to help us and our families survive. Through *altruism* we help others without any benefit to ourselves, even sometimes at a cost to ourselves, in order to create a better society that is more likely to help us back when we really need it. *Reciprocal altruism,* or helping another with the understanding that they will help you another time, is the foundation of many friendships and explains why trust is such an important component of close relationships. Research has also demonstrated that we find altruism attractive, which probably contributes towards explanations of why hero/ine stories are so popular.[6]

Related to altruism, *conscience* may have evolved as a way of forming alliances with larger groups. By being driven to act on our knowledge of what is morally right, we create a better world more conducive to our own survival as well as the survival of our relatives.[7] Within fiction, characters' altruism and conscience motivations have been used to powerful effect. Stories about these motivations typically deal with the consequences of a dangerous threat to humanity and demonstrate the powerful effects that people can have on their communities when they do the right thing and behave in selfless ways, sometimes placing their lives in danger in the process. A few examples of film protagonists motivated by altruism or conscience are included in Table 4.4.

Table 4.4 Evolutionary motivations relating to forming friendships and alliances

Motivation	Film	Protagonist
Altruism	*Avatar* (2009)	Jake Sully
	The Iron Giant (1999)	The Iron Giant
	Schindler's List (1993)	Oskar Schindler
Conscience	*Avatar* (2009)	Jake Sully
	Hotel Rwanda (2004)	Paul Rusesabagina
	Schindler's List (1993)	Oskar Schindler

Creating a legacy and meaningful life

The fifth group of motivations relates to the ways in which we interact with our culture or larger world. One of these motivations is to leave behind a lasting *legacy* for generations to come. That could be an important idea, a collection of art, a way of life or even a company. Some evolutionary psychologists speculate that we may also be motivated to try and draw *meaning* from our lives and to construct some kind of personal philosophy that gives our lives a sense of purpose.[8] Table 4.5 illustrates how these motivations drive the protagonists of a few well-known films.

Table 4.5 Evolutionary motivations relating to building a legacy and leading a meaningful life

Motivation	Film	Protagonist
Legacy	*The Theory of Everything* (2014)	Stephen Hawking
	Malcolm X (1992)	Malcolm X
	Gandhi (1982)	Gandhi
Meaning	*The Tree of Life* (2011)	Jack
	Solaris (1972)	Kris Kelvin
	The Seventh Seal (1957)	Antonius Block
	It's a Wonderful Life (1946)	George Bailey

Why some motivations make characters more compelling than others

Imagine that while travelling on the bus you overhear three conversations. In the first, a man runs down the stairs from the upstairs deck and shouts to a friend that he's just escaped from a woman with a loaded gun. In the second, you overhear the bus-driver flirtatiously exchanging phone-numbers with another regular passenger. And in the third, a middle-aged businessman tries to persuade a colleague to switch to different accounting software. Do all these conversations interest you equally? My guess is no.

Behavioural scientist Daniel Nettle argues that some stories are naturally more appealing than others because they appeal to higher adaptive stakes. He theorizes that in order to get our attention, fictional stories must be intensified – or more dramatic – versions of the conversations that we have about real life. The more at stake for a character in a story, the more likely that story will seize our attention. Because we're primed to listen most attentively to stories that affect our self-preservation, stories which feature a protagonist who is fighting to survive should be most compelling and have the potential to appeal to the largest numbers of readers or audiences. This is likely to be one of the reasons why Action, Adventure, Sci-Fi, Fantasy, War and, to a lesser degree, Thriller films and novels have the potential to draw the largest audiences and readers. The appeal of Horror films and books is limited by the fact that many people find them too frightening.

Second to stories featuring life and death stakes in which the protagonist is primarily motivated by their fight for survival, evolutionary theory predicts

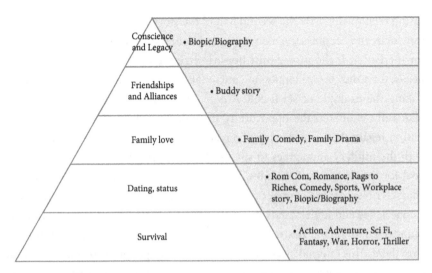

Figure 4.1 The relationship between a protagonist's primary goal, story genre and potential audience appeal.

that stories about dating and status competitions should also grab our attention, particularly when these are about situations in which competition is fierce, or the protagonist(s) stand a lot to lose. We are probably attuned to listening to these stories so that we can apply any strategies that we learn from them to situations in our own lives. Narratives falling into this category include Romantic Comedies, Romances, Sports stories, narratives set in the workplace and Biopics or Biographies about high status individuals and celebrities. Beyond these genres, as the stakes for a story's protagonist diminish, we would expect the size of the potential audience to fall. This relationship between a protagonist's primary motivation, story genre and the narrative's potential audience appeal is illustrated in Figure 4.1.

From external goal to internal need

One widely taught idea about character motivations is that the protagonist should start their journey driven by a conscious, external goal that provides their momentum for the first half of the story. This external goal, for example, the desire to become a multimillionaire, is in conflict with the protagonist's internal, unconscious or subconscious 'need', for example, to develop more caring relationships. By the second half of the story, the protagonist's need rises into focus and becomes the main force that both motivates and transforms them for the better. If the protagonist doesn't seize the opportunity to act on their needs, then they are generally on course for an unfulfilled life of unhappiness.[9] Taking the example of sci-fi epic *Avatar* (2009), when paraplegic protagonist Jake Sully is offered the opportunity to undergo a procedure that will allow him to regain the use of his legs, he readily agrees. In return, he aligns himself with the military and agrees to spy on the Na'vi. This becomes his motivating goal for the first half of the film. But when Sully then falls in love with Na'vi character Neytiri, and embraces all that life has to offer on Pandora, he develops a conscience and understands that rather than help the US military continue to plunder Pandora and destroy the Na'vi's way of life, he must, instead, try and stop them. This internal 'need' motivates Sully throughout the second half of the film. In this example and many others, the idea that a protagonist's goals must change from an external conscious desire to an internal 'need' seems to work, but from a psychological perspective, what is a 'need'? And is this transformational journey just a widely received Western formula linked to individualistic notions of heroism? Or could it be, as I will argue, that this commonly seen narrative pattern reflects the typical changes in motivational drives that occur across the human life course?

According to Self-Determination Theory, as we grow older we learn to fulfil three essential needs. These are as follows: to become more *competent* in negotiating different environments, to become more *autonomous* or capable of making independent decisions, and *to belong* by developing meaningful relationships with others. If we are exposed to positive social and cultural contexts then we usually achieve these needs, and are rewarded with greater well-being and happiness.[10] Research demonstrates that at the beginning of our life journeys, through childhood and into early adulthood, our goals tend to be *extrinsic*, which means that they are usually motivated by the possibility of receiving external reward. We're driven by the desire to make gains in life, acquire more power and more freedom,[11] and throughout this period we develop competence and autonomy. As our culturally valued extrinsic goals become associated with higher self-esteem, we typically internalize these goals and they become *intrinsic motivations* in later life.[12] Our midlife period is typically a time of reassessment of our goals – just like the midpoint of many narratives. During later life, our motivations shift from the more future-oriented goals of early adulthood towards spending time in more meaningful relationships and on personally meaningful goals in order to ensure that we have satisfied our final need – to belong.[13]

Drawing this all together, the widely taught idea that a protagonist's motivations usually change from being externally driven goals to internal 'needs' reflects the pattern of motivational change that we typically see in real life when people are exposed to positive social environments. The external motivations that drive many protagonists through the first half of their stories are usually agentic goals focused on acquiring more resources. From an evolutionary viewpoint, if the protagonists' survival isn't threatened, then these goals are often related to finding a partner or raising their status. Reflecting our midlives, the midpoint marks a period of reflection on these external goals, while the need comes more into focus. During the second part of the narrative, protagonists tend to be motivated more by internal or intrinsic motivations, which often relate to the need to belong. From an evolutionary perspective these motivations may fall under the categories of family love, forming more meaningful friendships and alliances, creating a legacy and more meaningful life, which all relate to our need to make connections with others. Table 4.6 brings all these points together in order to illustrate how the fictional protagonist's changing goals reflect motivational changes in real life.

Table 4.6 How the protagonist's changing goals reflect motivational changes in life

Act I – Midpoint Early adulthood	Midpoint – Act III Later life
External (extrinsic)	Internal (intrinsic)
Driven by external reward	Driven by greater self-esteem
Future-oriented	Present-oriented
	Pleasure-oriented
Acquiring things	Valuing what they already have
Greater competence and autonomy	Belonging
Dating	Family love
Developing / displaying physical skills	Forming friendships and alliances
Developing / displaying mental skills	Altruism
Improving / displaying appearance	Conscience
Acquiring wealth	Creating a legacy and meaningful life
	Other culturally valued goals

Sources: Ryan, Richard M. and Edward L. Deci. 'Self-determination theory and the facilitation of intrinsic motivation, social development, and well-being.' *American Psychologist* (2000); Freund, Alexandra M., Marie Hennecke and M. Mustafic. 'On gains and losses, means and ends: Goal orientation and goal focus across adulthood.' *The Oxford Handbook of Human Motivation* (2012).

Internal conflict

Conflicting motivations, thoughts, feelings and beliefs are central to the transformational change in motivations that we have just been looking at. These occur because our motivations, emotions and cognitions act independently on our neural circuits. For example, we may know that we need to tell the truth about a difficult situation, but feel fear at the prospect of doing so, so our feeling of fear censures our actions. Bearing the weight of our conflicting drives is an essential part of the human condition. When confronted with competing motivations we need to make choices about how we should act, faced with the knowledge that by making some gains there are others things that we stand to lose and that this will impact the way that our lives will unfold ahead of us. In the example of protagonist Valery Legasov from the TV miniseries *Chernobyl* (2019), sometimes the weight of those decisions is unbearable.

Short- and long-term motivations

Like people, well-written and complex characters are rarely motivated by just a single goal. In addition to long-term, overarching *distal goals* that power them through the narrative, they also have short-term, *proximal goals* that drive their actions from scene to scene. A character may be motivated by a longer-term desire to solve a crime (using their mental skills), while simultaneously trying to stay safe, explore a new environment (curiosity), and keep an affair with a love interest alight. By forcing a character to follow multiple goals, we develop the complexity that we expect from life and build tension as we complicate the narrative and increase the gap between our hopes for the character (to solve the crime, stay safe and realize the love affair) and our fears for them (failing to solve the crime, getting hurt in the process and losing their love interest). Sometimes the shorter-term goals also serve as a way of getting the protagonist to achieve their longer-term goal. Interestingly, but also not surprisingly, people are more likely to continue to pursue a personally meaningful long-term goal if they envisage the series of interconnected short-term steps that they need to take along the way.[14] Having your protagonist develop a plan and reveal it to the audience, therefore, isn't just a lazy way of communicating plot and keeping the reader on track with their progress, it's a natural technique that many successful people use.

Revealing character through their decisions

Some writing theorists suggest that it is only by putting our characters under pressure that we reveal their true selves. 'True character is revealed in the choices a human being makes under pressure – the greater the pressure, the deeper the revelation, the truer the choice to the character's essential nature', writes Robert McKee in his seminal text *Story* (1999). This idea that we have an essential nature is both interesting and complex. We've already seen that personality is best captured by the five-factor model, which shows our dispositions towards acting in certain ways. But since we behave differently with different people, in different situations, is it right to say that we're at our most authentic when we're under pressure? Probably not. Most people report feeling most true to themselves when they're feeling calm, content, loving, free,[15] 'in the present'[16] and behaving in socially desirable ways.[17] But if, instead, by essential nature McKee means behaving in our most primal and instinctive ways, then he's right. The choices that we make under the greatest pressure – when our lives are threatened – are entirely instinctive and out of our conscious control. Emotions of panic, fear or rage converge in our unconscious minds, triggering our survival instincts. In these most threatening situations, we typically act in one of two different ways. While the *fight-or-flight* response appears to be more characteristic of men, studies suggest that in times of great stress women are more likely to *tend-or-befriend*.

In fight-or-flight, the more characteristic male response to fear, there are not two but four distinct responses that appear sequentially in response to a threat and are more complex than they might sound. The first of these is to *freeze*, a response which creates time to monitor the situation and avoid detection. The next response is an attempt to *flee*, and if this is unsuccessful it is followed by an attempt to either *fight*, or display verbal aggression or use other active coping mechanisms to get out of danger. For writers, this creates some interesting options to reveal character. Is your character more likely to launch into a violent attack, shout threats or use some kind of other clever but equally confrontational strategy in order to try and extract themselves from danger? Finally, if this fight response is still unsuccessful then another instinct kicks in – playing dead, otherwise known as *tonic immobility*.[18,19]

In the tend-or-befriend response that appears to be more characteristic of women in highly threatening situations, two responses are frequently observed. The first involves self-nurturing or tending to children that may be close by, in order to reduce stress and promote safety. The second instinctive response is to reach out and befriend strangers who may be able to help in this dangerous time, or to foster relationships with existing friends.[20] If these are the typical ways in which we are instinctively motivated to react towards the most dangerous threats, how do we choose how to react in situations that are less dangerous? When situations are highly emotionally charged but not life-threatening, we're more likely to take risks in our decision-making and underestimate how dangerous those risks are. One emotion that we might experience in these situations is anger, which simplifies our decision-making process and makes us more likely to draw on stereotypes.[21] In situations that are less emotional, we usually act on 'gut feelings', thinking back about how well things have gone in the past when we've made similar decisions.[22] We then use these memories to make predictions about what is likely to happen for each of the options open to us, while also assessing how likely we are to be able to pull off these various possibilities.[23] The result is our emotionally informed decision.

Thinking about this in relation to protagonist Valery Legasov in the TV miniseries *Chernobyl* (2018), when early in the series he is called to a meeting at the Kremlin, he has to decide whether or not to be the one to explain that the core of the nuclear reactor must have melted, threatening the lives of millions. There are presumably no comparable situations that Legasov has ever had to face in his life, and as an introvert, having to assert himself and point out others' flaws in the assessment of the nuclear reactor leak to the most powerful people in the Soviet Union, he finds himself frozen and unable to speak. It is only when Gorbachev announces that the meeting is adjourned, that Legasov realizes that he can't wait any longer and forces himself to speak up.

Drawing it all together

Motivations breathe life into our characters, give them direction, motivate plot and sow the seeds of conflict. Evolutionary psychology suggests that motivations fall into five groups, relating to survival, finding a partner, family love, forming friendships and alliances, and creating a legacy and meaningful life. Of these motivations, stories about survival have the highest evolutionary stakes and for this reason are most likely to seize our attention and have the potential (if well-written) to appeal to the largest audiences.

At the centre of most fictional narratives is a protagonist who is faced with competing motivations, emotions and thoughts. Reflecting life, they usually begin their stories motivated by a conscious external goal, which often relates to becoming more independent, acquiring things, improving their status or finding a partner. The midpoint of the narrative is typically a turning point in which the protagonist reassesses these external goals. At this point their need to feel more connected with others usually comes into focus. This need for connection with family, friends or other alliances often drives the second half of the story. In some stories about highly generative or particularly heroic protagonists, the need for connection may also lead the protagonist to create a legacy and more meaningful life. So, while protagonists' goals are generally selfish and agentic, their needs are typically to forge closer connections with others. Your protagonist may need to repair fractured relationships, build on new relationships, or allow themselves to fall in love.

Once you've nailed your main character's major motivations, it's time to think about the other major characters in your narrative. What is it that your antagonist wants, and how does this create a major obstacle for your main character? Similarly, what are the goals of your other main characters? How do these differ from those of your main character? Which goals are broadly shared, and which others create further conflict? Also consider how your characters will set about trying to achieve their objectives. If they are particularly ordered and conscientious they may make plans, breaking down each step towards their goal into a series of sub-goals. Or if they are more spontaneous characters they may wander through life in a far more carefree manner, less focused on making any achievements.

By this point you should have a pretty good understanding of how your characters are likely to want to act. You'll have a general idea of where your story is going and the obstacles that your main character is going to face along the way. These obstacles play a significant role in the way that most characters change. We've already begun to consider how characters transform in relation to their motivational changes. In the next chapter we'll dig deeper and uncover when, why and how else characters transform.

5

When, why and how characters transform

Change is an inevitable and constant part of life. We are born, we grow older and we die, while around us seasons pass, our environments transform, and our cultures evolve. As we grow older, we also develop and transform as individuals. We learn new skills, acquire greater knowledge and are changed by life events good and bad. Through these changes we gain new perspectives on life, new beliefs about what is important, and new motivations. Even our personalities, or our essential selves, evolve. These changes are a fascinating part of our lives that help us draw meaning from our lived experiences and shape our identities. These changes are also central to the vast majority of fictional narratives. In this chapter we'll be examining when, why and how fictional characters typically transform and how this mirrors the growth that we typically experience in our own lives.

When people change

One of the ways in which we all transform is by growing older. Over the last forty years, psychologists and psychiatrists including Dan McAdams, Daniel Levinson, George Vaillant, Roger Gould and David Gutmann have argued that human development follows predictable life stages. In so doing they follow earlier frameworks developed by Carl Jung, Sigmund Freud and Erik Erikson. Psychologists tend to group these transitional periods in our life into around five chapters. First there is *childhood*, then *adolescence, early adulthood, the mid-life period*, and then *later life*. Each of these chapters in our life is characterized by different central concerns or themes that become important. For writers, it is useful to better understand these themes because they often inform stories about characters in different life stages. Let's take a look at what typically happens at each stage.

Childhood (five to twelve years)

One of the main concerns for children in this age group is to become *competent*. As they acquire a whole variety of new skills, their self-esteem rises steadily until the age of eleven.[1] One of these skills is to see the world through other people's eyes. When this skill develops, children begin using social comparisons to define their sense of self and consider how they are going to make it in this world.[2] Meanwhile, friendships, particularly with others of the same sex, become increasingly important. To illustrate these changes, Table 5.1 includes examples of well-known child protagonists whose major transformation relates to learning new skills and becoming more competent.

Table 5.1 Examples of transformations of child protagonists

Film/Novel	Protagonist	Transformation
Inside Out (2015)	Riley Andersen	Learns to understand the role of her emotions
Home Alone (1990)	Kevin McCallister	Learns that he can look after himself (but still needs his parents)
Matilda (Dahl, 1988)	Matilda Wormwood	Learns to use her powers
Lord of the Flies (Golding, 1954)	Ralph	Learns about the human capacity for evil

Adolescence (thirteen to nineteen years)

For the majority of teenagers, these years are centred on *finding their identity*. In order to do this, teens typically explore different identities until they settle with one that feels most right for their emotional needs, goals and values. Loyal and intimate friendships become more important as teens start to hang out in peer groups, which may have their own unique values and identities. These groups play a vital role in social support as teens become more independent from their families.[3] During this period teenagers also start to construct meaning from life through personal narratives that weave together their experiences.[4] By way of illustration, Table 5.2 includes examples of how adolescent fictional protagonists' transformations often relate to explorations of their identity.

Early adulthood (twenty to thirty-nine years)

Now comfortable with their newly found sense of identity, this is the stage in which many young adults learn to navigate their first serious relationships, and

Table 5.2 Examples of transformations of adolescent protagonists

Film/Novel	Protagonist	Transformation
Lady Bird (2017)	Christine 'Lady Bird' McPherson	Gains a more complete sense of her identity
Mean Girls (2004)	Cady Heron	Explores different school cliques until she is comfortable with her identity
The Secret Diary of Adrian Mole, Aged 13 ¾ (Townsend, 1982)	Adrian Mole	Finding his identity, friendships and relationships
The Catcher in The Rye (Salinger, 1951)	Holden Caulfield	Learns that the alienation he feels as he explores his identity will eventually pass

locate themselves in the world of work. Many people in this stage will be driven by the *desire for power and freedom* and trying *to make gains* in their life. At the beginning of this period they may also be dealing with serious *responsibility* for the first time[5] and may already be starting to think about their legacy. Throughout early adulthood, young people's self-esteem continues to rise, most steeply until the age of thirty.[6] Table 5.3 includes some examples of the transformations of early adult protagonists in well-known films and novels related to increasing responsibilities and the desire to make gains.

Table 5.3 Examples of transformations of early adult protagonists

Film/Novel	Protagonist	Transformation
The Wolf of Wall Street (2013)	Jordan Belfort	Makes and then loses his fortune
The Devil Wears Prada (2006)	Andrea Sachs	Grows in confidence at work
The Secret History (Tartt, 1992)	Richard Papen	Learns to take control of his own life
The Bell Jar (Plath, 1963)	Esther Greenwood	Learns how to free herself of her fears and pressures upon her

Midlife (forty to sixty-four years)

The midlife period is for many people a time of *turmoil and transition*. It's a pivotal period at the intersection of growth and decline.[7] As later life approaches, people typically review whether life has turned out the way they imagined it, whether they have met the goals they had been aiming for, and whether these are

Table 5.4 Examples of transformations of protagonists in midlife

Film	Protagonist	Transformation
Birdman Or (The Unexpected Virtue of Ignorance) (2014)	Riggan Thomson	Gains validation through critical acclaim
Thelma And Louise (1991)	Thelma Dickinson and Louise Sawyer	Gain independence and freedom
Break of Day (Colette, 1928)	Colette	Learns to be happy without love
Mrs Dalloway (Woolf, 1925)	Clarissa Dalloway	Learns to accept her life as is

the same goals they want to follow for the rest of their lives. If this is sounding a lot like the midpoint in many fictional narratives, then you'll now understand the reason why. During midlife, people often start to think more about how they can become more 'generative', through creating more meaningful connections with other people, helping others in society and also creating some kind of legacy that they will leave behind.[8] For many people, midlife is a stressful time which may involve additional responsibilities at work,[9] the need to care for children and aging parents, and a time in which aspirations align with reality. Many studies have shown that happiness and life-satisfaction reach their low point at midlife,[10] but not everyone follows this trajectory. The midlife crisis is a ubiquitous stereotype that appears to affect only 10 to 20 per cent of (American) adults around this age.[11] For highly active and generative people, midlife is often a high point in their lives, when they balance their conflicting desires for personal *agency* (the need for status, dominance and control) and *communion* (the desire for connectedness, warmth and love) and achieve many great things.[12] Whether or not people are feeling happier in their lives, their self-esteem continues to rise until the age of sixty.[13] Table 5.4 includes some examples of well-known fictional protagonists who experience a period of turmoil or reassessment in their midlives.

Later life (sixty-five years onwards)

In this last stage of life people are generally concerned more with conserving and maintaining what they have rather than gaining new things or skills. Earlier in this period people enjoy their friendships, and find more meaning in the present. Happiness increases during this period and stress decreases.[14] Towards the end of life, people often look back and reflect on whether they feel they've lived a good life and made the right choices. Integrity comes with feelings of

Table 5.5 Examples of transformations of protagonists in later life

Film/Novel	Protagonist	Transformation
Amour (2012)	Georges Laurent	Maintains integrity by fulfilling a promise to his wife
The Best Exotic Marigold Hotel (2011)	Evelyn	Finds her independence
Up (2009)	Carl Fredricksen	Fulfils a lifelong dream
The Old Man and The Sea (Hemingway, 1952)	Santiago	Accepts the natural order of life

accomplishment, but despair may accompany the feeling that life goals and happiness haven't been achieved. Table 5.5 includes some examples of well-known fictional protagonists in their later lives who have either chosen to fulfil a lifelong dream, or found another way of maintaining their integrity.

Why people change

Having discovered when people typically change, we are now going to look at other reasons why people change. You won't need this book to tell you that we are shaped by our life experiences. Some of the most significant and meaningful events in our lives are also very emotional. We can be transformed in positive ways by an emotional high point, otherwise known as a *peak experience*. A *traumatic event* may leave us feeling frightened and distressed. When we master a particularly difficult challenge we may experience our subsequent feelings of empowerment as a *turning point*. Psychologists have found that these life-changing events help explain how someone changes, or remains the same, over time.[15] In the best fiction, these are the emotionally extreme moments that connect character with plot.

At the same time as creating a structural framework for our stories, they define the most important moments in the protagonist's emotional journey. Through their emotional resonance they also re-engage audiences and readers with the character.

Peak experiences

Peak experiences are the high points in someone's life. They are moments that bring intense joy, inner peace, the feeling of being alive, transcending oneself

Table 5.6 Examples of film protagonist transformations brought about by peak experiences

Film/Protagonist	Peak Experience(s)	Transformation
Avatar (2009)	Bonds with the direhorse	Fully appreciates life
Jake Sully	Rides the ikran for the first time	Connects with the
	Initiated as a member of the Na'vi	Na'vi
	Listens to the voices of the ancestors	Finds meaning in
	Pair bonds with Neytiri	his life
A Beautiful Mind	Realizes his mathematic formula	Regains his life and
(2001)	Wins the Nobel Prize	career
John Nash		
Chariots of Fire (1981)	Runs in various races	Overcomes his feelings
Harold Abrahams	Wins an Olympic gold medal	of inferiority

or experiencing one's full potential.[16] These kinds of experiences are often accompanied by the feeling of loss of time and/or place. Some people experience these high points when looking at awe-inspiring natural scenery. For others the triggers may be sexual love, childbirth, extreme sports, religious moments, scientific insights, viewing art, creative work or moments of introspection.[17] These experiences are reported to change people's lives for the better by increasing their feelings of well-being and making their lives feel more meaningful.[18] By way of illustration, Table 5.6 includes examples of the transformations brought about by protagonists' peak experiences in a few well-known films.

Low points

The emotional low points in our life stories are equally important in shaping the way that our lives unfold. While the majority of people recover well from stressful life events by putting these down as useful learning experiences, and a few experience positive psychological growth, when events are particularly frightening or distressing people may go on to develop depression, anxiety or post-traumatic stress disorder (PTSD).[19] These could include being victims of a violent assault, sexual abuse, injurious accident, losing a loved one, witnessing a violent death, seeing a family member being injured or dying, diagnosis of a life-threatening condition, experiencing a natural disaster, being involved in military combat, or being held hostage. Around a third of people experiencing one of these events will develop PTSD. This means that they relive the traumatic episode through flashbacks or nightmares, typically avoid situations that

Table 5.7 Examples of film protagonist transformations brought about by low points

Film/Protagonist	Low point	Transformation
Leave No Trace (2018) Thomasin Mckenzie	Evicted from her (family) home in a state park	Learns she must make her own choices in life
Manchester By the Sea (2016) Lee Chandler	Losing his children in a fire in their family home	Begins his recovery from PTSD by arranging to continue his relationship with his nephew
The Theory of Everything (2014) Stephen Hawking	Diagnosis of motor neurone disease	Throws himself into his work and experiences positive psychological growth

remind them of the event, and may also experience isolation and guilt. For some people, PTSD develops immediately after the distressing event, but for others –including when related to childhood abuse – PTSD may not unfold for months or even years.

Recovery generally involves slowly rebuilding trust with other people through friendships, or taking on a job and engaging in hobbies, and is supported by trauma-focused therapy.[20] Personality also plays an important contribution in our recovery from life's most difficult events. Psychologists have found that people who are more emotionally stable, higher on agreeableness, openness and extroversion, are more likely to experience positive psychological growth after a traumatic event. This might include having a greater appreciation for life, greater optimism, increased happiness and well-being and deeper relationships with others.[21] In Table 5.7 we explore how the low points of protagonists in some recent films have been instrumental in their character transformation.

Turning points

The turning points in our lives are the events that we feel significantly change us. They often relate to events that have enabled us to move from dependency towards autonomy and may be points at which we've had to make major decisions. These kinds of events include self-mastery, acquiring a higher status, a significant achievement, taking on a major responsibility or empowerment. Other turning points involve gaining a profound insight into our lives which may relate to our identity.[22] Through this insight, we may find new goals or missions in life.[23] A number of examples of these turning points for the protagonists of a few well-known films are included in Table 5.8.

Table 5.8 Examples of film protagonist transformations brought about by turning points

Film/Protagonist	Turning point	Transformation
Leave No Trace (2018) Tom	Returning to the community without her father	Living life for herself
Thelma And Louise (1991) Thelma and Louise	Deciding to go on the run	Feeling empowered for the first time
The Karate Kid (1984) Daniel	Mastering the impossible kick	Experiencing a sense of accomplishment

How people change

Having looked at when people typically change and why they might change, we're now going to look at how people change. This change affects three different aspects of our characters. As we grow older our *personality* matures; the nature of our *motivations* transforms; and our *beliefs* are shaped by our life experience and moral development. In the sections that follow, we'll look at each of these processes in more detail.

Personality development

Although personality is generally described as stable, it actually develops and matures through our lifetime. The Big Five dimensions start to emerge from early childhood,[24] and by their late teens, young adults have developed a more stable personality. As we grow older, we generally become more emotionally stable, more extrovert, more open and more agreeable until these traits peak in midlife. As we age further, we become a little more neurotic, introverted, closed to experience and disagreeable. Throughout our lives, we also become increasingly conscientious.[25] The increase in conscientiousness and agreeableness may help explain why we become more oriented towards the need for belonging and connectedness as we grow older, and why we are more likely to take part in communal activities that benefit others.[26]

Motivational change

In the previous chapter we saw that our early adult lives are typically dominated by selfish, *agentic* desires related to *making gains*, and acquiring more *power*

Table 5.9 Examples of film protagonists' motivational changes

Film	Protagonist	Initial agentic goal	Later communal goal
Dallas Buyers' Club (2013)	Ton Woodroof	To make money selling an antiretroviral drug	To help LGBT members of his club
Avatar (2009)	Jake Sully	To make money and regain the use of his legs	To help the Na'vi keep their homeland
Erin Brockovich (1993)	Erin Brockovich	To make money	To help her clients win the settlement they deserve
Schindler's List (1993)	Oskar Schindler	To get cheap Jewish labour for his factory	To save his workers from being put to death

and *autonomy*. Our midlife period is a period of reassessment of these goals. As we grow older we typically become more motivated by more *communal* goals including the need to *belong*, and develop more meaningful *relationships* with others, and if we are particularly generative then we may also be motivated by the need to build a *legacy* we feel proud of.[27] So, the general pattern of motivational change is from more selfish to more selfless goals, reflecting the typical change in protagonists' motivations that we see in the vast majority of Western stories. In Table 5.9 we take a look at some examples of these typical motivational changes in the protagonists of well-known films.

While the majority of research into motivational changes has focused on WEIRD populations (Western, Educated, Industrialized, Rich and Democratic), research into human moral development suggests that the general trend of becoming less selfless and more concerned for others as we grow older is probably a universal.[28] This isn't to say that everyone experiences this journey, nor that everyone goes through the same degree of motivational transformation as they age. Exposed to the right life opportunities, some people become particularly generative towards others as they grow older – for example the titular character in *Schindler's List* (1993). Other people change far less, but their motivational changes are generally still in the same general direction as we have outlined. So, for example, in the American biographical comedy-drama film *Green Book* (2018), protagonist Tony Lip is initially motivated by his pay cheque to take the job of a driver for Dr Don Shirley. As the film progresses, he starts to overcome his racist attitudes, bonds with Dr Shirley and becomes closer with his wife.

Although his motivational changes are less pronounced, the general pattern that we've seen, from more selfish to selfless. It is also interesting and worth noting that the motivational changes that play out throughout our whole life course are typically compressed in films and novels into the story time, which may run from a number of years to just a few months or sometimes even days. That's quite some change!

Changing beliefs

As we are changed by our life experiences, our beliefs about the world may adjust accordingly. Our beliefs are also shaped by the people we meet along the way, major transitions in our life, and major events happening around us. Since people's choices and actions are influenced by their beliefs, what a character believes, how this influences their actions, and how their beliefs are changed by the events of the narrative are important factors for writers to consider. Let's take a look at some of the most useful psychological research in this field that might help the creation of more compelling characters.

Our early beliefs about the world are influenced by those of our family and other important caregivers. Children of highly politicized parents typically share the same political views as their parents.[29] Similarly, children of religious parents who have good relationships with their parents are also more likely to share their religious orientation.[30] By contrast, people who are more open to experience are more likely to engage in a whole variety of different ideas and be more open to accepting new ideas about the world. And as we might expect, people who are more closed to experience are far less likely to consider ideas that they aren't already familiar with and are therefore more conservative in their outlook.[31]

There are several reasons why people may change their beliefs. First, if their environment or lived experience is incongruent with their beliefs,[32] and their actions bring about negative consequences which make them feel bad.[33] A second reason why people change their beliefs is by developing a relationship with someone whom they like and trust but who holds different views from theirs.[34] When holding those new beliefs is found to be a rewarding process, this positive feeling makes it more likely that these new beliefs are internalized.[35] For protagonist Jake Sully in *Avatar* (2009), meeting his love interest Neytiri provides him with the opportunity to see the world of Pandora through her eyes. Taking on her more spiritual views brings the meaning and purpose that he had said was lacking in his life, so it makes complete sense when we see Sully then begin to act on these new beliefs.

A third reason why people's beliefs may change is that an intense emotional experience causes them to re-evaluate their attitudes or even life philosophy.[36] Trauma survivors who experience positive psychological growth often report that after their recovery they find it easier to relate to others, see new possibilities, live every day to its fullest, and try to enjoy life more. For some people going through intense emotional experiences, their religious beliefs are strengthened, while others become more cynical and less religious.

Drawing it all together

The typical patterns of character transformation that we see in many longer-form works of fiction, in novels, films and TV series, closely reflect the natural changes that we experience in our own lives. Some of these changes relate to the different stages of our life: childhood, the teenage years, early adulthood, midlife and later life. Through these stages we first acquire skills, become more competent and autonomous, and explore our sense of identity. We then pursue goals related to making gains and take on responsibilities. At the midpoint of our lives we typically reassess whether the direction in which our early-life motivations have taken us is where we want to be, and then later in life pursue more communal goals. These life stages reflect our motivational changes, from more agentic to more communal goals as well as our personality changes, as we become more conscientious and more agreeable until late in life. In addition to these developmental changes in our lives, we are also changed by emotionally intense life events in the form of peak experiences, low points and turning points. These change our beliefs, provide the structure to our lives and stories, and give them meaning. They are the events that we invoke in explanations of who we are, and who we have become. In the same way that we make sense of our own lives through explanations of how we have handled the things that have happened to us, we also draw meaning from the way that characters learn from the events in their fictional lives.

Table 5.10 provides a summary of the major changes in motivation, happiness, self-esteem and personality through adulthood which informs the journeys of many fictional characters.

Table 5.10 Major changes in motivations, happiness, self-esteem and personality throughout adulthood

Early adulthood (20–39 years)	Midlife (40–64 years)	Later life (65 years onwards)
Agentic motivations	Reassessment of motivations	Communal motivations
Making gains	Aspirations aligned with reality	Developing more meaningful relationships
Acquiring more power and autonomy	Coping with additional responsibilities	Building a legacy
Living for the future		Enjoying the present
Increasing happiness	Least happy	Increasing happiness
Rising self-esteem	Rising self-esteem	Decreasing self-esteem
Becoming more emotionally stable, extroverted, agreeable and conscientious	More conscientious Emotional stability, extroversion and agreeableness peaks	More conscientious and a little more neurotic, introverted, closed to experience and disagreeable

Sources: McAdams, Dan P. *The redemptive self: Stories Americans live by – revised and expanded edition.* Oxford University Press (2013); Freund, Alexandra M., Marie Hennecke and M. Mustafic. *On gains and losses, means and ends: Goal orientation and goal focus across adulthood.* The Oxford Handbook of Human Motivation (2012); Specht, Jule, Boris Egloff and Stefan C. Schmukle. 'Stability and change of personality across the life course: The impact of age and major life events on mean-level and rank-order stability of the Big Five.' *Journal of Personality and Social Psychology* (2011); Orth, Ulrich, Ruth Yasemin Erol and Eva C. Luciano. 'Development of self-esteem from age 4 to 94 years: A meta-analysis of longitudinal studies.' *Psychological Bulletin* (2018).

In this chapter we have already uncovered why emotionally intense life events in the form of turning points, peaks and low points create the structure of most fictional narratives. In the next chapter we'll go on to investigate how these events are woven together to create the protagonist's emotional journey and why emotions, including those induced by fiction, have the potential to exert such a powerful force on human behaviour.

The emotional journey

Storytelling is an emotional experience. Whether we're writing stories, reading novels, watching films or listening to a radio play, our emotions are engaged. Depending on our mood, we seek out different genres of fiction and we're probably better at writing different kinds of scenes. There are times when we want to forget a hard week, sit back and be entertained, there are times when we want to laugh, and there are times when we want to feel moved, or try to make more sense out of life. Different forms of fictions offer us all of these emotional possibilities as well as many more through providing us with characters who we care about, who we invest in and who take us with them on rich emotional journeys.

Emotions exert an immensely powerful influence on human behaviour. They organize and guide the way that we see the world, they shape our memories, they guide our relationships and they steer the choices we make. In this chapter we'll investigate how a better understanding of the process of emotional engagement with a character can help writers develop more compelling characters. We'll examine the six basic universal emotions as well as a few other emotions that are particularly powerful for storytellers. We'll learn why characters who experience a wider variety of these emotions are more compelling and we'll explore the six most common emotional story arcs. Finally, we'll take a closer look at how stories end.

How we empathize with a character

Early researchers believed that cinema audiences come to identify with fictional characters through the processes of empathy and *emotional contagion*, in which an emotionally expressive character triggers similar emotions in the viewer.[1] *Mirror neurons*, which fire when we watch someone performing an action, were thought to explain this process of emotional contagion, but recent research suggests there's little evidence to support that this is actually the case.[2] A further problem is that the theory of emotional contagion isn't sufficient to explain why we don't empathize with characters whose actions we judge as being morally wrong. In order to address this problem, cognitive psychologists Dolf Zillmann and Joanne Cantor theorized that audiences form emotional biases towards characters according to their moral judgements about them. In their *Affective Disposition Theory*, Zillmann and Cantor suggest that viewers experience pleasurable feelings when good protagonists are rewarded by positive narrative outcomes and antagonists are punished with negative outcomes.[3] In other words, we enjoy stories that reflect our everyday feelings about a 'just world'. Feel free to skip ahead if that's enough theory for you, but if you're interested in understanding why an audience's subjective judgements about the moral virtues of a character are important, read on.

Evolutionary biologist Robert Trivers discovered that human relationships are built on a sophisticated system that regulates our *moral emotions*. This includes the development of friendships with the people who are most likely to help us, as well as avoiding or punishing people who cheat. Back in our ancestral environment these skills would have been very important in enhancing our chances of our survival, and the survival of our families. Trivers proposed that our moral emotions, including love, compassion, gratitude, admiration and elevation developed in order to develop vital friendship groups while other moral emotions, including disgust and moralistic aggression, developed in order to keep us safe from people who may harm us.[4] Our moral emotions explain why we empathize with characters who we perceive to be good, why we engage with them, why we are moved by their emotional journeys, and why we want their actions to be rewarded by positive outcomes. We root for protagonists whom we trust and who – if they were real – would be good prospects as friends. Furthermore, the more similar that we perceive a character to be to ourselves, the more deeply we are moved by the narrative.[5] One of the most commonly used techniques that helps readers identify with a character is by showing them dealing with an everyday obstacle in a relatable way. Let's take a look at the way that screenwriter Phoebe Waller-Bridge does this in the introduction to her *Fleabag* (2016–19) pilot.

```
INT. FLEABAG FLAT. CORRIDOR. NIGHT. 1

Shot of the inside of a front door. Fleabag's POV.
```

Shot of Fleabag a few steps away from the door, watching it as if she's ready to pounce. Smudged makeup, hair tousled. Out of breath.

Shot of the inside of a front door. Fleabag's POV. Shot of Fleabag. She turns to the camera.

FLEABAG
(Earnest, touch of pain)

You know that feeling when a guy you
like sends you a text at 2 o'clock
on a Tuesday night and asks if he can
'come and find you' and you accidentally
make it out like you've just got in
yourself, so you have to get out of
bed, drink half a bottle of wine, get
in the shower, shave everything, put
on some agent provocateur business,
suspender belt, and wait by the door
until the buzzer goes -

(buzzer goes)

And then you open the door to him like you'd
almost forgotten he was coming over.

Excerpt from 02/03/2015 shooting script for the pilot of *Fleabag* (1989). Written by Phoebe Waller-Bridge. Courtesy: Two Brothers Pictures / BBC.

So how is it that we come to identify with the character of Fleabag through this introduction? First, many readers among the show's target audience will identify with the awkward and highly inconvenient social expectations around the situation that Fleabag finds herself in. Second, the way in which the character tells her story is funny, which makes her a more likeable character. It demonstrates that she cares about social relationships and wants to engage with them. Part of Fleabag's humour is in her disarming honesty. By trusting the audience, the character encourages us to trust her in turn – an essential quality in positive relationships. Humour is also an attractive quality: it's a sign of intelligence, and also a good coping strategy, which are appealing attributes in someone that we're considering spending time with. In summary then, we rapidly identify with

Fleabag because she appears to be someone who experiences life in a similar way: she appears to be trustworthy and charismatic. We, of course, also engage with her because she is entertaining.

Our moral emotions also explain why we are so good at spotting characters whom we don't trust, why we feel little if any sympathy for antagonistic characters, and why we want villains to be suitably punished. Our moral emotions explain why our feelings about fictional characters rarely change from the moment they are formed. So, when characters whom we like perform in ways that we consider to be somewhat immoral, we tend to *morally disengage*[6] – in just the same way that we overlook the times when our friends act in ways that we disapprove of. Our moral emotions also account for why we side with somewhat unlikeable protagonists when the other characters around them are even less trustworthy. As readers and audiences, our relationships with fictional characters are proxies for the real human friendships and relationships that we form. We make the best choice of friends that we can – fictional or otherwise – from the characters that we're presented with.

Putting aside the theory, let's consider the example of protagonist Mildred Hayes from the American independent drama *Three Billboards Outside Ebbing, Missouri* (2017). When first introduced, it would be hard to describe her as sympathetic or likeable. Instead, she's blunt, disagreeable and entirely consumed by her own needs. However, when we then learn that her single aim is to find justice for her daughter who was raped while dying, we realize that rather than being self-centred, Mildred is, instead, on a selfless mission to do the right thing. Her blunt ways are immediately redeemed and from here on we see her as good and entirely deserving of our sympathies.

Personality and emotions

Psychologists have found that our personality plays a big part in the way that we experience the world. While extroverted people are generally more happy, enthusiastic, active, confident, energetic and sociable, introverts experience more neutral emotions and tend to be more quiet, reserved and aloof. This means that the extrovert's emotional experience of the world is altogether different from the introvert's. For extroverts, socializing with other people is a rewarding experience that makes them feel happy. By contrast introverts feel more comfortable when alone or with just one or two people whom they are close to. Neuroticism is another personality dimension to play a major role in the way that we feel about the world. People who are more emotionally unstable are more prone to emotional ups and downs, as well as more anxiety. Since they tend to be more sensitive, they are typically more likely to feel hurt, or take offence when things don't go their way. That may lead to prickly feelings, or anger. By contrast people who are more emotionally stable have a much calmer outlook on life, rarely feeling ruffled and enjoying stable moods.

When we talk about the different ways in which people experience the world, which emotions are we referring to? How many emotions are there, and which of these are most important to writers? In the sections to follow we'll take a closer look at the universal emotions, what these are and why they are so important to consider when we're developing fictional characters.

The six basic universal emotions

The idea that some emotions are universally expressed has been around for hundreds, if not thousands of years. In 1872, Charles Darwin observed that young people and old people, from different cultures, express the same states of mind through the same movements. These emotions, he hypothesized, and the way in which they are displayed must be innate. Nearly a hundred years later, American psychologist Paul Ekman set out to discover if he was right. Travelling to Papua New Guinea, he showed pictures of faces expressing different emotions to the isolated and preliterate Fore people. When he asked them which emotions they would display in certain situations, he found that they picked out the same six emotions that his North American test subjects did – *Anger, Fear, Disgust, Happiness, Sadness* and *Surprise*.[7] He concluded that these six basic emotions are displayed on the face, recognized and interpreted across cultures in very similar ways, and that they must have evolved to help us deal with basic life tasks. On a side note, it is no coincidence that five of these emotions – Anger, Fear, Disgust, Joy and Sadness – were anthropomorphized in the 2015 Pixar film *Inside Out*. Ekman was a consultant on the film. The sixth emotion surprise was apparently dropped by director Peter Docter because he felt that the storyline was stronger through using just five emotions. Returning to our main subject, let's take a more detailed look at each of these six basic emotions in turn.

Anger

Anger is one of our most primitive emotions and plays an important part in our survival. It is one of the ways in which we have adapted to fight off threats, compete for resources and reinforce social norms, by standing up for what we believe is right. Anger results from a mismatch between what we've learned to expect from a situation and the reality of what happens. The degree to which we experience anger depends on the situation, our personality, age and life experience. The closer the friend who upsets us, the more likely we are to feel angry and hurt. This is particularly true for adolescent girls.[8] People who are more disagreeable and neurotic but less conscientious are more likely to express anger.[9,10] Older adults tend to express anger outwardly less frequently than younger adults and children, seemingly because they are better at using calming strategies to regulate their emotions.[11]

In terms of story dynamics, anger is a powerful motivating force. We saw this earlier in the example of Mildred Hayes from *Three Billboards outside Ebbing, Missouri*. Her anger at the lack of police action towards finding her daughter's rapist and murderer motivates her entire journey. Feeling anger tends to make us more impulsive, confident and reckless. It also makes us more likely to underestimate the chances of something going wrong.[12] Equally powerful is the uglier side of anger – it makes us feel more negatively towards people outside our own group and more likely to look for someone to blame.[13]

Fear

Fear is another of our most primitive emotions that plays an important role in our survival. As we saw in Chapter 4, in some situations fear prompts us to try and escape from danger as rapidly as possible, while in other situations we may try and fight, tend to children or befriend others who may be able to help. Given that fear encompasses deeply unpleasant feelings of terror, why do many people appear to enjoy frightening episodes in stories? Some scholars believe that one reason is the vicarious thrill that we experience when reading about or watching a character faced with a dangerous situation respond in an adaptive way and survive. Since our minds have evolved to reward us when we behave in ways that benefit our survival, we experience the same euphoric highs when watching a character make a good decision in a frightening situation that allows them to survive.[14] Another theory, the *ordeal simulation hypothesis*, argues that fictional stories about high risk but rare threatening events allow us to train our responses to best deal with these situations should they ever happen to us.[15] Frightening stories may act as simulations of ordeals through which we are able to see the outcomes of different actions that we could take.

Although many difficult situations in our lives provoke some fear, we mostly learn to overcome these. More emotionally stable people sail through these somewhat frightening and difficult situations more easily. In the previous chapter we touched on the role that fear may play in a character's transformation when they go through trying life events. When a character perceives a traumatic situation to be particularly terrifying and out of their control, based on real-life outcomes we would expect them to be more likely to experience long-lasting anxiety and depression as well as PTSD. By contrast, if a character experiences a potentially traumatic situation as less frightening, more within their control, and feels as though they have handled the situation well, they are more likely to recover well from it and possibly even experience post-traumatic growth.

Disgust

Another of our most ancient emotions, disgust is thought to have evolved as a way of protecting us from pathogens that might give us infection. These could include pathogens in certain foods, or those in people carrying an infectious disease.[16] Although disgust plays a vital role in our survival, it also contributes towards *xenophobia* and some people's dislike for members of other groups. People who are more sensitive to disgust tend to find their own group more attractive and have more negative views about other groups.[17] The other two forms of disgust are *sexual disgust* and *moral disgust*. We feel sexual disgust towards potential partners or acts that we find unattractive, while moral disgust relates to our dislike of acts that we see as immoral. Although disgust has evolutionary roots, because it is also shaped through social conditioning, different cultures have aversions towards different foods, sexual practices and social behaviour. North Americans, for example, are more likely to experience moral disgust towards actions that limit an individual's rights, freedom or dignity, while Japanese people are more likely to be disgusted by actions that restrict their integration into the social world.[18]

Disgust can be a highly revealing part of the way that fictional characters are portrayed. Apart from grave moral wrongs, little else disgusts Tyrion Lannister from *A Song of Ice and Fire* (Martin, 1996–)/*Game of Thrones* (2011–19). He is open to experience, sexual practices and interested in the ideas of other groups. For other characters in the series, including Cersei and Daenerys Targaryen, disgust at other people's moral transgressions, particularly if they are members of another group, is motivation enough to kill.

Happiness

Happiness encompasses a broad range of feelings, from *amusement* through *contentedness* to *euphoric joy*. Psychologists believe that these pleasant feelings have the important function of allowing us to broaden our awareness about the world around us, and encourage new exploratory thoughts and actions.[19] Taking for example, Jake Sully, the paraplegic protagonist of *Avatar* (2009), the euphoric joy that he experiences when he runs in his avatar form for the first time appears to contribute towards opening up his mind to the extraordinary world of Pandora around him and, with this to new ideas about the Na'vi. When particularly intense, positive emotions may become the peak moments or high points of a character's emotional journey, as we saw in Chapter 5, these peak experiences have the potential to be just as transformative as a character's low points.

Sadness

Sadness is another emotion that plays a universal and inevitable role in the human experience. Characterized by emotional pain, it is associated with feelings of *loss, disadvantage, despair, grief, helplessness* or *sorrow*. These feelings turn our attentions inwards, probably as a way of giving us time out from our usually busy lives so that we can come to terms with our loss, take stock and revise our goals and plans. From the perspective of writing a fictional character, sadness is an immensely useful and important emotion for just that reason. If a character's emotional pain is significant, this low point in the storyline may lead them to reassess their plans and revise their strategies. Low points often also play a vital role in character transformation, as we saw in the previous chapter.

Low points aren't just useful in the way that they align a character's emotions with the plot, they also intensify readers' and audiences' experience of feeling moved.[20] Some researchers believe that we enjoy moving stories because they provide us with a safe environment in which to learn about how a character deals with a difficult event that we may have experienced ourselves, or which we may go through in the future. This may provide us with insights into how to better handle such events, or give us a chance to try and draw some meaning from them.[21]

Surprise

Surprises may be good, bad or neutral and may vary in their intensity, from indifferent feelings to intense reactions that provoke the fight-or-flight response. The greater the gap between our expectations of what is going to happen and what actually happens, the greater the surprise. Since we frequently ignore weak signals about surprising events that are to come,[22] in order to feel convincing, surprises or narrative reversals should be set up well in a story in a way that we wouldn't spot on first reading or viewing, but in a way that becomes clear should we review the narrative again. For example, on first viewing of the supernatural drama *The Sixth Sense* (1999), the audience is misled into thinking that the narrative is being objectively rather than subjectively narrated by Malcom, the main character, because we follow scenes from the points of views of other characters and not just Malcolm. Despite this, the film's surprise ending still manages to feel coherent and psychologically convincing because the emotional perspective through which we've engaged with the film remains the same. We experience the same shock and catharsis as Malcolm, and the surprise ending works. On a second viewing of the film, we spot the weakly communicated signals about Malcolm's death that we may not have seen before, including that he is the subjective narrator.

Further universal emotions

A few years after proposing his basic list of six, Ekman expanded his list to include a wider range of emotions that are not all expressed through the face. Other psychologists have also added to this list by providing evidence for the following emotions as universal: *amusement, awe, contempt, contentment, desire, elevation, embarrassment, guilt, interest, jealousy, love, pain, pride, relief, satisfaction, shame, sympathy* and *tension*. Rather than outlining the psychological mechanisms behind all these emotions, we'll just take a look at four which may be particularly useful to writers when developing characters. These are elevation, awe, shame and tension.

Elevation

If you've ever watched a film or read a novel in which the main character performs exceptionally kind, brave or virtuous acts that leave you with distinctive feelings of warmth and being moved, uplifted, and inspired to do good deeds yourself, then you've experienced the emotion known as elevation (also referred to as moral elevation). Feelings of elevation can be triggered by watching people perform acts of charity, compassion, kindness, love, self-sacrifice, courage, forgiveness, loyalty, or any other strong virtue which is experienced as an act of 'moral beauty'.[23] Watching or reading about others performing these acts can be an incredibly powerful experience that has been shown to reset the mind, erase pessimistic or cynical feelings and replace them with hope, love and moral inspiration. As writers, if you're interested in creating a narrative that shakes up and inspires people's lives, then elevation is undoubtedly the single most important emotion in your repertoire. Table 6.1 includes a few examples of film protagonists whose actions of moral beauty had the potential to evoke feelings of elevation among the audiences watching these films.

Table 6.1 Examples of film protagonists' actions inspiring elevation

Film	Protagonist	Act inspiring elevation
Winter's Bone (2010)	Ree Dolly	Shows courage and loyalty towards her family
Hotel Rwanda (2004)	Paul Rusesabagina	Saves Tutsi refugees at his hotel
Forrest Gump (1994)	Forrest Gump	Shows exceptional kindness and loyalty
Schindler's List (1993)	Oskar Schindler	Shows courage, compassion and self-sacrifice when he saves Jews from Auschwitz

Awe

Sometimes described as an overwhelming feeling of reverence, admiration and connection to the universe, awe may be evoked by power and vastness. Feelings of awe often cause us to have new insights about our life and our place in the world. Like elevation then, awe is another powerful emotion for writers who want to inspire or evoke change in their readers and audiences. Awe-inspiring moments include gazing at vast natural scenes, having a spiritual encounter, listening to a powerful and charismatic leader, listening to awe-inspiring music

Table 6.2 Examples of film protagonists who are shown to experience moments of awe

Film	Protagonist	Awe-inspiring scene
Blade Runner 2049 (2017)	K	Epic opening scenes
The Theory of Everything (2014)	Stephen Hawking	Invents his theory about black holes
Avatar (2009)	Jake Sully	Listens to the voices of the ancestors beneath the Tree of Souls
Into the Wild (2007)	Christopher McCandless	Gazes at the epic view from the top of a mountain he's climbed
Close Encounters of The Third Kind (1977)	Roy Neary	Sees the aliens emerge from the mother ship Says goodbye in the final scene
2001: A Space Odyssey (1968)	Dr David Bowman	Throwing the bone sequence The Stargate sequence

or even understanding or inventing a grand theory.[24] These positive experiences of awe are related to meanings of the word *awesome*, but there is also another category of awe-inspiring experiences which are related to fear or great apprehension and sometimes described as *awful*. These experiences that bring on feelings of powerlessness as well as dread may be triggered by gazing at the cosmos, watching a powerfully frightening natural phenomena, or encountering the face of God.[25] Table 6.2 includes a few examples of moments from films when the protagonists have experienced positive or negative feelings of awe.

Tension

There's no need for me to point out that tension, and its close relative suspense, is one of the most important emotions for writers to learn to master. The appeal of many stories, films, television series, radio plays and novels is often directly related to the level of tension that they create. From a psychological perspective, tension results from *states of conflict, instability, uncertainty* or *dissonance*, in which the reader is asked to hold two opposing beliefs at once about something that is emotionally significant (this emotional significance is key). These states trigger the reader to predict what's going to happen next, and to yearn for the instability or tension to be resolved. Interestingly, these identical principles apply to music as well as stories – just reflect on the soundtracks typically used in moments of high suspense and you'll find them characterized by dissonant or unstable sounds that we yearn to hear resolved.[26] Linked with this resolution of tension is the promise of reward by the brain's pleasure centres as well as the potential to learn from the social situation depicted in the story.[27]

At this point you may well be wondering why we're discussing tension in a book about characterization, when tension may seem mostly related to plot. And here's why: in order to create suspenseful stories, your audience need to *care* about what's going to happen in your story. To do that, they need to feel so emotionally invested in your character that they develop hopes and fears for them. Researchers Lehne and Koelsch theorize that the greater the gap between these hopes for the very best outcome for a character and fears for their worst-case scenario, the greater is the tension developed.[28]

The 2019 television miniseries *Chernobyl* is a master class in developing tension for the screen. First, it provides us with several convincing and sympathetic lead characters in whom we invest emotionally. Then it shows how the lives of these characters, as well as those of several million others, are placed at significant and almost incalculable risk. The gap between our hopes and fears for these characters is vast, and millions of lives are potentially at stake. The fact that the series is based on the real-life events of the catastrophic nuclear accident at the Chernobyl power plant in 1986, and that much of what actually happened was covered up at the time, further adds to its tension. Also essential in keeping the audience hooked is the tension that builds throughout the story. Initial attempts to clean up the site don't work. Estimates of the dangers involved in failure to clean up the site increase. As a result, the audience is placed in increasing states of cognitive conflict until the ending of the series is reached.

Shame

Shame and guilt are self-punishing acknowledgements that we've done something wrong which goes against social norms. Although guilt is usually associated with the feeling that we need to make amends for our actions, or at least confess our guilt, shame tends to provoke feelings that are more related to wanting to insulate ourselves from our actions, by hiding away, disappearing or escaping. Similarly, while people who experience guilt are often inclined to wish that they had acted differently, people who feel shame tend to feel they had little control over the event and blame it on the way that they are.[29] A far more potent and distressing emotion, shame is a feeling that we can also experience vicariously through others, particularly when we see ourselves as having a shared social identity.[30]

This means that the closer we identify with a fictional protagonist, and the more similar that we see ourselves to them, the greater we experience the protagonist's shame. Taking, for example, protagonists Eva and Jan from Ingmar Bergman's 1968 Swedish drama *Shame*, the closer we grow to them as the narrative unfolds, the more we feel their sense of shame as war presses them into performing actions that they would never have considered otherwise.

Emotional range

Understanding how single emotions can be more powerfully used is just one part of understanding how to create more emotionally engaging characters. Equally important is the knowledge that readers appear to enjoy experiencing a full range of emotions when immersed in a narrative and that this appears to motivate them to pay continued attention to the story.[31] If we consider just an average day in real life, we're typically pulled through a whole range of emotions in our interactions with family, colleagues, strangers and friends. On most days these are probably mild emotional experiences, but they are still rich and varied, spanning interest, amusement, irritation, disappointment, guilt and pride. Given that most fictional protagonists' emotional journeys appear to be intensified versions of the range of emotions that we experience in our day-to-day lives, and that this may be a requisite in order to create a story that takes readers' attention away from their real-world experiences, it is hardly surprising that when confronted with fictional stories that are less emotionally engaging, we read these as emotionally 'thin', 'boring' or 'one note'.

Let's take a look at the range of emotions that writer-director James Cameron takes his protagonist Jake Sully through in *Avatar* (2009). Sully's journey isn't confined to just emotional peaks and troughs. His emotional experience includes the full range of emotions that we see in Table 6.3. And although I can't yet prove it, I suspect that this emotional range contributes significantly towards the film's commercial success.

Emotional arcs

In 1945, while studying for his Masters in Anthropology, American writer Kurt Vonnegut made an intriguing observation: stories could be classified

Table 6.3 Example scenes demonstrating the range of emotions displayed by the protagonist in *Avatar* (2009)

Emotion	Example scene
Anger	Watches Quaritch's army destroy the Home Tree
Fear	Is attacked by a thanator
Disgust	Learns that Quaritch plans to destroy the Home Tree
Happiness	Runs through Pandora for the first time
Sadness	Watches Grace die
Surprise	Watches the Helicoradian retract when touched
Amusement	Mistakenly crashes his tail into a table when first inhabiting his avatar
Awe	Listens to the voices of the ancestors beneath the Tree of Souls
Contempt	Watches Quaritch's army destroy the Home Tree
Contentment	Lies with Neytiri after making love
Desire	Makes love to Neytiri
Elevation	Listens to dying Tsu'tey as he hands over his leadership to Sully and asks to be set free
Embarrassment	Falls off the direhorse
Guilt	Works for Quaritch while befriending Neytiri
Interest	Learns to control his avatar's body
Love	Pair bonds with Neytiri
Pain	Gasps for breath in the shack during the film's climax
Pride	Rides the Toruk
Relief	Breathes again when Neytiri places the gas mask over his face, saving his human form
Satisfaction	Successfully controls his avatar's body for the first time
Shame	Admits to the Na'vi that he knew Quaritch's plans all along
Sympathy	Feels for all the Na'vi when their Home Tree is destroyed
Tension	Anticipates the threat posed by Quaritch's plans to destroy the Home Tree

into categories according to the rise and fall of fortune of their protagonist. He suggested that 'stories have shapes which can be drawn on graph paper, and that the shape of a given society's stories is at least as interesting as the shape of its pots or spearheads'.[32] Although Vonnegut chose to explain the five story forms that he subsequently identified as describing the protagonist's changes in fortune against time, his graphs could equally be considered as showing the valence of the protagonist's emotions over time since people are generally happier when they experience good things in life, and less happy when their fortunes change. Vonnegut named the five story forms that he identified Man in a Hole, Boy Meets Girl and a version of it, the Cinderella story, Creation Myth, and Kafka's Metamorphosis. Of these, he noted that Creation Myths tend to be limited to religious stories of the creation of the world, and Kafka's Metamorphosis is a very unusual story form. Our focus, instead, will be on the most popular story forms.

Following in Vonnegut's footsteps in 2011, Professor of English and Data Analytics Matthew L. Jockers set out to investigate the truth behind Vonnegut's claims that all stories could be classified into categories according to the emotional rise and fall of their narratives. Using a technique called sentiment analysis, which measures the positive or negative valence of every word in a text and then plots these along a timeline, he found that the emotional arcs of the nearly 5,000 novels that he analyzed are dominated by just six basic shapes.[33] They are *Tragedy, Rags to Riches, Man in a Hole, Quest, Cinderella*, and *Oedipus*,[34] which I outline in the sections that follow. This is not to say that all stories in films, plays or novels follow these emotional arcs, since many are more complex, but that these are the most common. It is equally important to note that these arcs show the highly smoothed average changes in emotion across six major story forms that were identified. The arc of any individual novel that was analyzed would likely deviate from these averages in many places. These six emotional story arcs therefore shouldn't be taken as precise templates to follow when writing, but as informative guides. In the immediate sections that follow we'll be looking at the broad changes of emotions across the whole storyline that result from a macro level of analysis. Later, we'll be taking a closer look at the emotional curves in stories that happen at the micro level. These reveal the changes in emotion from scene to scene.

Tragedy (fall)

In the Tragedy storyline, illustrated in Figure 6.1, the main character starts the story with good fortune – or feeling positive – then encounters a series of increasingly difficult events that leave them feeling very low by the end of the narrative. They experience a small change in fortunes for the better at the beginning of the second act, and then another downturn or reversal in fortunes at the midpoint. In other Tragedies, the protagonist's fortunes simply go from good to bad. For example, in Tom Wolfe's 1987 novel *Bonfire of the Vanities*, the central character Sherman McCoy starts the book as a successful New York bond trader and self-proclaimed Master of Wall Street. After he is involved in a hit-and-run event, his life spirals downhill. By the end of the novel he is penniless, estranged from his wife and daughter, and awaiting trial for manslaughter. Typical to the Tragedy, Sherman starts off the story with good fortune, which then takes a turn for the worst when he encounters difficulty. In some Tragedies

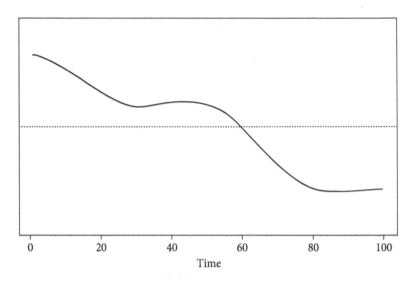

Figure 6.1 Emotional arc of the Tragedy.
Source: Jodie Archer and Matthew L. Jockers, **The Bestseller Code** (Penguin Press, 2017.)
Copyright © Jodie Archer and Matthew L. Jockers, 2016. Reprinted by permission of Penguin
Books Ltd. Reprinted by permission of Trident Media Group in the US and its territories, Canada
and the Philippine Islands.

the story's resolution is defined by a small upturn in the protagonist's emotions
at the resolution, at the point where they start to come to terms with their loss,
and in others the line charting the protagonist's increasingly tragic fate is almost
entirely flat.[35]

Other examples of tragic novels include the 2015 Pulitzer Prize winner and
New York Times bestseller *All the Light We Cannot See* (Doerr, 2015), *The Devil
Wears Prada* (Weisberger, 2003) and *Rainbow Six* (Clancy, 1998). Films following
this emotional story form include *Love Story* (1970), *Monty Python and the Holy
Grail* (1975), *Toy Story 3* (2010), *Life of Pi* (2012) and *Get Out* (2017).[36]

Rags to riches (rise)

The *Rags to Riches* arc (sometimes referred to as the Comedy within literary
criticism) takes the opposite trajectory to the Tragedy. As illustrated by
Figure 6.2, the protagonist starts the narrative with poor fortune and then a series
of increasingly good things happen to them. For example, in the well-known
children's novel *Charlie and the Chocolate Factory* (Dahl, 1964), protagonist
Charlie Bucket begins his journey in poverty, with his grandparents. After

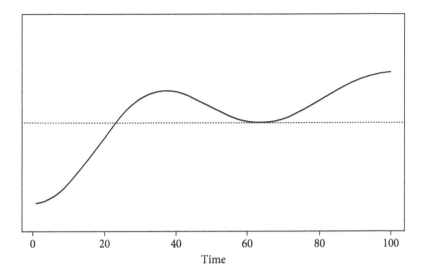

Figure 6.2 Emotional arc of the Rags to Riches story.
Source: Jodie Archer and Matthew L. Jockers, **The Bestseller Code** (Penguin Press, 2017.) Copyright © Jodie Archer and Matthew L. Jockers, 2016. Reprinted by permission of Penguin Books Ltd. Reprinted by permission of Trident Media Group in the US and its territories, Canada and the Philippine Islands.

winning a golden ticket he is awarded a tour of Willy Wonka's famous chocolate factory. Because of his singularly good behaviour throughout the tour, Charlie learns that he will be Wonka's successor to the chocolate factory. Often in Rags to Riches stories, the middle act is defined by a small downturn in the protagonist's fortune as they encounter an obstacle that they have to overcome.

Other novels with the Rags to Riches arc include *The Divine Comedy* (Dante, 1308–20), *Madam Bovary* (Flaubert, 1856), *The Client* (Grisham, 1993) and *The Secret Life of Bees* (Kidd, 2001), while films include *Pretty Woman* (1990), *The Shawshank Redemption* (1994), *Slumdog Millionaire* (2008), *The Social Network* (2010) and *The Favourite* (2018). In films, this emotional arc is most commonly associated with biopics and historical plots.[37]

Man in a hole (fall–rise)

In the *Man in a Hole* story form, illustrated by Figure 6.3, the narrative typically begins with an everyday protagonist experiencing quite a comfortable life. Things then take a turn for the worst when the protagonist falls into a metaphorical hole from which they have to dig themselves out in order to recover their fortunes.

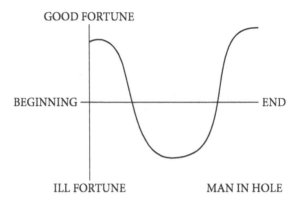

GOOD FORTUNE

BEGINNING ———————————————————— END

ILL FORTUNE   MAN IN HOLE

Figure 6.3 Emotional arc of the Man in a Hole emotional story.
Source: K. Vonnegut, **A Man Without A Country** (London: Bloomsbury, 2007) © K. Vonnegut, 2007, A Man Without A Country, Bloomsbury Publishing Plc.

By the end of the story the protagonist is typically happier than at the beginning of their journey, usually because they've developed resilience through their experiences and may see life in a more meaningful way. In the previous chapter we looked at how difficult life experiences can result in this kind of positive developmental growth.

Stories with the Man in a Hole emotional arc include the world's first recorded story, the *Epic of Gilgamesh* (c. 2100 BC), the European fairy tale *Little Red Riding Hood* (c. seventeenth century), *The War of the Worlds* (Wells, 1898), *Dracula* (Stoker, 1897), *The Silver Linings Playbook* (Quick, 2008)[38] and the overall storyline for the *Harry Potter* series (Rowling, 1997–2007). Films following this story form include *The Godfather* (1972), *The Departed* (2006), *Life of Pi* (2012), *12 Years A Slave* (2013) and *Mary Poppins Returns* (2018). Research suggests that the most financially successful films released in the West have screenplays that follow this emotional arc, even when the film's production budget and genre are controlled for.[39]

Quest (rise–fall–rise–fall)

The Quest emotional arc is almost the inverse of Man in a Hole but with an additional complication around the midpoint of the narrative. As its name suggests, this emotional arc is most commonly associated with stories about protagonists exploring new worlds, defeating some kind of metaphorical or literal monster, and then returning home. As Figure 6.4 illustrates, at the

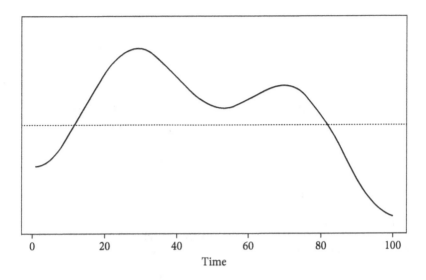

Figure 6.4 Emotional arc of the Quest story.
Source: Jodie Archer and Matthew L. Jockers, **The Bestseller Code** (Penguin Press, 2017.)
Copyright © Jodie Archer and Matthew L. Jockers, 2016. Reprinted by permission of Penguin
Books Ltd. Reprinted by permission of Trident Media Group in the US and its territories, Canada
and the Philippine Islands.

beginning of this story the protagonist experiences a rise in fortune, but then
encounters some kind of difficulty at the end of the first act. By the midpoint,
the protagonist has generally found a way of solving or getting around this
problem and their fortunes rise again, only to encounter another major
difficulty in the third act. This usually leaves them in a worse position or
feeling more depressed about life than when they started the journey. A more
common rise–fall emotional arc in films has the protagonist experience an
upturn in feelings at the end of their quest, showing that life has become less
bleak at the end of the story, perhaps because they've had a chance to learn
something from their journey.[40]

Novels following the rise–fall–rise–fall emotional arc include *The Corrections*
(Frantzen, 2001), *The Satanic Verses* (Rushdie, 1988) and *Love the One You're
With* (Giffin, 2008),[41] while films with a general rise–fall pattern include *On the
Waterfront* (1954), *Mary Poppins* (1964) and *A Very Long Engagement* (2004).

Cinderella story (rise–fall–rise)

Just like the Cinderella fairy tale that it is named after, in this emotional arc
something wonderful happens initially to the protagonist, their fortunes then

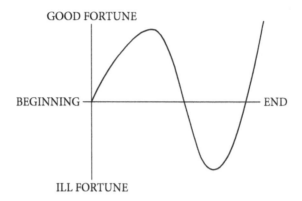

Figure 6.5 Emotional arc of the Cinderella story.
Source: K. Vonnegut, **A Man Without A Country** (London: Bloomsbury, 2007) © K. Vonnegut, 2007, A Man Without A Country, Bloomsbury Publishing Plc.

change for the worse, before finally changing again for the better. In some stories following this general form the protagonist is happier at the end of the narrative than they were at the beginning, generally because they have a greater appreciation for their relationships as well as life in general. These are storylines in which we see the protagonist experience positive growth after difficult events or loss. In other versions of this story form the protagonist's fortunes change for the better at the end of the narrative, but don't recover to the level that they were at the beginning. Novels with this general rise–fall–rise arc include *Misery* (King, 1987), *Big Little Lies* (Moriarty, 2014) and *Testimony* (Shreve, 2008),[42] while films include *Rushmore* (1998), *Spider-Man 2* (2004)[43] and *Can You Ever Forgive Me?* (2018).

Oedipus (fall–rise–fall)

In the *Oedipus* emotional arc, the protagonist's fortunes initially fall, then rise, and then fall again. In other words, they initially experience some great misfortune leading to an emotional low point. After this their fortunes pick up, but are marred once again as we see in Figure 6.6. Novels following this fall–rise–fall emotional arc include *Fifty Shades of Grey* (James, 2011), *Wolf Hall* (Mantel, 2009)[44] and *Frankenstein; or the Modern Prometheus* (Shelley, 1818), while films include *The Little Mermaid* (1989), *As Good as it Gets* (1997), and *All About My Mother* (1999). Films following this story arc are often within the sports genre.[45]

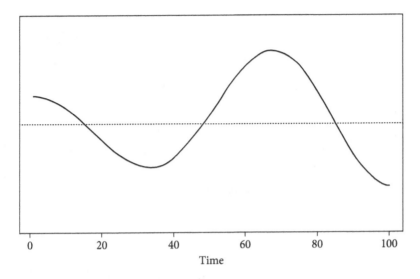

Figure 6.6 Emotional arc of the Oedipus story.
Source: Jodie Archer and Matthew L. Jockers, **The Bestseller Code** (Penguin Press, 2017.)
Copyright © Jodie Archer and Matthew L. Jockers, 2016. Reprinted by permission of Penguin
Books Ltd. Reprinted by permission of Trident Media Group in the US and its territories, Canada
and the Philippine Islands.

Page-turners

While the macro level of sentiment analysis tells us about the protagonist's
broadest changes in emotions from the beginning to the end of the narrative,
it doesn't tell us about the emotional fluctuations that occur from page to page
or from scene to scene. Analyzing these micro level changes in sentiment,
Matthew L. Jockers and Jodie Archer discovered that novels that were page-
turners shared a common emotional form. They took their readers through a
rollercoaster of regularly rising and falling emotions. Their frequent turning
points were steep, symmetrical and regularly spaced. In other words, the
narratives of these stories appear to capture their readers' attention because
of these rhythmic and constant changes in the protagonist's fortunes.[46]
Just as events appear to be going well for the protagonist, their fortunes
change completely, keeping readers continuously on their toes. From a
psychological perspective, it's likely that the cyclical nature of the tension –
reward cycle in which the protagonist repeatedly faces relatively high stake
threats and then is rewarded for making adaptively successful decisions –
creates an intoxicating and even somewhat addictive experience for the reader.

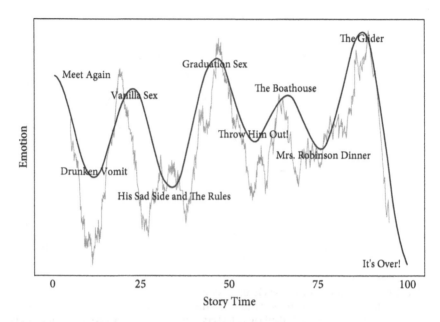

Figure 6.7 Emotional peaks and low points in *Fifty Shades of Grey* (James, 2011). *Source*: Jodie Archer and Matthew L. Jockers, The Bestseller Code (Penguin Press, 2017.) Copyright © Jodie Archer and Matthew L. Jockers, 2016. Reprinted by permission of Penguin Books Ltd. Reprinted by permission of Trident Media Group in the US and its territories, Canada and the Philippine Islands.

Figure 6.7 is a reproduction of a graph showing the results of sentiment analysis performed by Archer and Jockers for the bestseller *Fifty Shades of Grey* (E. L. James, 2015). The lighter grey lines show the emotional fluctuations from scene to scene, reflecting the moment-by-moment conflicts between protagonists Ana and Christian. When these curves are smoothed by the computer, they graph the major turning points of the novel, shown by the bold black line. Note how quickly their fortunes change between their emotional peaks and troughs, creating that feeling of a rollercoaster of emotions for the reader.

How the story ends

All stories have to end, but how they end can feel satisfying or unsatisfying. Endings that we experience as satisfying typically bring about a resolution of the narrative's main tensions. Inter- and intra-personal conflicts are resolved, unstable states returned to stability, and any conflicting ideas that were presented are now reconciled. For the audience, this resolution of tension triggers the neural reward circuits, bringing about positive emotions and the feeling that this narrative journey has been a satisfying experience. Equally important to the ending that we experience as satisfying is that the story's characters are shown to reap their 'just rewards'. Protagonists whom we have judged to be good are fairly rewarded, while antagonists are appropriately punished. Taking, for example, *The Wizard of Oz* (1939), the end of the film sees Dorothy returning home, rewarded for being a good friend to others by being reunited with Toto, her dog, and surrounded by family and friends who love her. When she declares that she will never have any need to leave home again it is evident that she has learnt that she has everything here that she needs. The main tension of the storyline is resolved – Dorothy is reunited with Toto, other storylines are tied up and the result is a satisfying and upbeat ending.

Of course, in real life there are many occasions when 'good people' are not fairly rewarded, 'bad people' get away with their acts, and tensions remain unresolved. Fictional narratives that choose to reflect the reality of the human condition give readers and audiences a chance to reflect on the meaning of life. Rather than offering escapism, they offer a safe space for us to contemplate life as it really is. Thinking, for example, about Michael Haneke's critically acclaimed psychological drama *Caché* (2005), one of the film's major themes is how oppression results in unresolved societal tension, which is aptly reflected at the film's ending in which the major storyline lacks a firm resolution.

The happy ending

The happy ending has become a characteristic so readily associated with Hollywood films, and particularly those produced within the classical period of filmmaking (1918–60), that the happy endings are often referred to as Hollywood happy endings. During the era of the Motion Picture Production Code in the United States, law enforced that film narratives must follow a strict moral code, and happy endings were encouraged. While some researchers might argue that the Hollywood happy ending has arisen from the legislative and cultural pressures that originated in the era of the Production Code, an alternative explanation is that we are hard-wired for optimism.

The *optimism bias* is the pervasive human phenomenon through which people feel unrealistically optimistic about their future and underestimate the likelihood of experiencing negative events.[47] The majority of us think that we're likely to live longer, healthier and easier lives than we likely will.[48] Some evolutionary psychologists believe that this optimism bias evolved as a way of convincing others that we're good candidates for acts of reciprocal altruism, that is, friendship. Other researchers suggest that the function of our optimism is to give us hope in the knowledge of our own mortality.[49] Whatever its basis, our innate optimism bias may help explain why many people prefer positive, redemptive stories, in which bad events are 'made good' through positive outcomes[50] and tensions are resolved. Thus, far from being the artificially imposed cultural and historical construct that some researchers have suggested, stories with happy endings may well reflect a deep truth about our human nature.

The tragic ending

If humans are hard-wired for optimism and often prefer redemptive stories with happy endings, then why do people 'enjoy' tragic dramas, melancholy novels or heart-wrenching operas? As we have already touched on several times, melancholy stories or narratives, in which good is not shown to always come from difficult events, provide us with a more realistic view of life. Readers of tragic novels and viewers of more melancholy films may choose these narratives because they provide them with the opportunity to grapple with questions about life's purpose, particularly around the subject of our mortality, in a safe environment.[51] By watching fictional characters struggling with life's challenges, we are reminded that these difficult moments are an essential part of life, so that we feel less alone when we experience similar ordeals ourselves. Tragic endings also give us the opportunity to learn from any poor choices that a protagonist may have made and which resulted in this ending, so that we can avoid making similarly poor decisions ourselves.

The mixed affect ending

Many well-known films, novels and television series have endings that are neither purely happy nor entirely sad. Take the ending of American drama *Thelma and Louise* (1991) for example, where the main characters avoid being captured by the police by driving their car off the edge of a canyon. On the one hand, the ending is, of course, tragic. The characters are fully aware that there's no way they are going to survive their final move. But on the other hand, the film's musical score and the exhilaration on Thelma's and Louise's faces signify freedom and triumph for the characters. For the audience, this ending evokes mixed emotions, combining feelings of sadness and hope. Together, these mixed emotions feel moving. Mixed emotions are often associated with endings, both in real life and in fiction, and are often accompanied by contemplation about life's biggest questions.[52] Knowing that something is coming to an end makes that experience feel more poignant, and even more so as we get older.[53]

Drawing it all together

It is through our emotions that we connect with stories. Narratives draw us in because we form an emotional connection with their characters. At the beginning of this chapter we looked at how audiences identify with protagonists whom they trust. We then examined the basic universal emotions – anger, fear, disgust, happiness, sadness and surprise – and how tension may be developed in a narrative by creating a gap between the reader's hopes for the protagonist, and their fears. We also investigated why positive emotions including moral elevation, joy and awe are so powerful in the hands of storytellers. We saw that stories in which characters experience a variety of emotions feel rich and emotionally compelling and we explored the six most common emotional arcs found in Western narratives. Finally, we considered the ending – why certain endings feel satisfying; why endings that don't resolve tension may still be right for your story, and what audiences take away from happy, tragic and mixed affect endings.

Now that you've understood your character's emotional journey, it's time to move on and think about your secondary characters. In the next chapter we'll uncover some fascinating research on human relationships that will allow you to better understand how your characters are likely to behave with others and why personality plays such an important role in our relationships.

Secondary characters

Stories are rarely told about a single character acting in isolation. They are about situations and relationships. Secondary characters drive stories forwards, provide alternative perspectives on the central theme, and create obstacles or support for the main character. They often force the protagonist to make choices, rethink plans and decide what's most important to them. Secondary characters also have a major part to play in the protagonist's emotional journey. Good friends, family or lovers may share the main character's peak experiences, and they may also be around for their low points. Just as our real-life relationships are dynamic, the most compelling and believable fictional relationships also shift and change. At different times we bring different motivations, different needs and different moods to our relationships, which change the nature of these interpersonal connections. Relationships may swing from being positive and supportive to being hostile and strained. One conversational poor turn as a result of a difficult day may take a relationship down an unforeseen rabbit hole, or an unexpectedly kind gesture from a new acquaintance could cement a lifelong friendship. Mastering the writing of these shifting dynamics so that they feel compelling and believable is an essential skill for longer-form storytellers. In this chapter we'll dig deep into the psychology of interpersonal relationships to uncover what we can learn that may be helpful in refining these skills.

First, let's consider whether secondary characters need to be written with the same levels of complexity as the main character in order to be convincing. Do secondary characters need to be characterized across all dimensions of the Big Five as well as their thirty facets of personality? Or are there shortcuts that we can and should make when writing them? Research tells us that in the first five seconds of meeting strangers, we make fairly accurate judgements about their levels of extroversion, and good estimates of their agreeableness, neuroticism, conscientiousness, negative emotions and even intelligence.[1,2] So in short periods of time, we probably don't read many more aspects of a stranger's personality unless they are engaged in an activity that clearly reveals a strongly expressed facet of their personality, for example, showing angry hostility. Despite this, we assume that when we meet a stranger for just a few seconds, they have as complex and fully rounded personalities as the people that we know best, but we just haven't had a chance to see these other aspects of their personalities. The same is very likely true of fictional secondary characters. Provided that they act in entirely convincing ways when we first meet them on at least a few dimensions, and particularly extroversion, this is generally enough to convince us that these persons are 'believable' for a short period of time. However, the more time we spend with any secondary character, the greater our expectations will be of seeing further complexity of their personalities. So, while flatter characters are useful, as E.M. Forster notes, because their consistency isn't a distraction from the main storyline, rounder characters, with whom we spend more story time, require deeper characterization. Depending on the length of story time that the reader will spend with them, this may mean drawing out your secondary characters in three, four or five dimensions, expressing their most memorable facets of personality, and giving them clear motivations and beliefs.

In the sections that follow we'll investigate how else psychological research can inform us in writing more believable and engaging character relationships. We'll start by looking at the Interpersonal Circumplex, which charts the main styles of relationships that people have with others. Next, we'll cast our eyes over the main functions that secondary characters typically fulfil, and what psychological research can usefully tell us about these roles. We'll also investigate how our personalities shape the kinds of relationships that we have with other people and how we can use this knowledge to create more convincing relationships between our fictional characters. When it comes to matters of the heart, we'll ask whether opposites really attract. Last of all, we'll dive deep into research that tells us how our personality affects the ways in which we try to get what we want. If this sounds interesting, then read on!

The Interpersonal Circumplex

Studying the ways in which we relate to each other, personality psychologists noticed that two of the Big Five dimensions, extroversion and agreeableness, play a particularly important role in interpersonal relationships. While

Extroversion captures the degree to which we are outward-facing and want to socialize with others, Agreeableness describes our warmth and our desire to get along with other people – two extremely important qualities in relationships. Developing this idea, American psychologist Mervin Freedman and his team proposed that the variety of ways in which people relate to each other may be conceptualized as falling within a circular model, which was later named the *Interpersonal Circumplex*. Within this circular model, one axis represents *agency*, which measures a person's need for status, dominance and control – think Cersei from *Game of Thrones* (2011–18). The other axis measures *communion*, which describes someone's need for connectedness, friendliness, warmth and love – think Samwell Tarly. So, as illustrated in Figure 7.1, every point within the Interpersonal Circumplex represents a weighted combination of needs for agency and communion.[3]

People and characters who fall near one of the poles on the Interpersonal Circumplex create the clearest impressions of agency or communion. In other words, they come across as particularly warm or cold-hearted, or very dominant or submissive. Other characters whose interpersonal styles fall

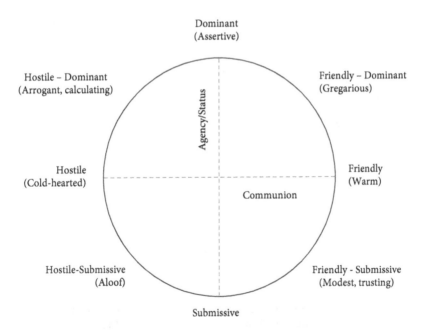

Figure 7.1 Capturing relationships using the Interpersonal Circumplex.
Source: J. S. Wiggins and R. Broughton, The interpersonal circle: A structural model for the integration of personality research. (1985) **Perspectives in personality**, 1, pp.1–47.

along the edge of the circle also send out stronger messages of dominance, submission, warmth or hostility. By contrast, characters whose interpersonal styles would be plotted right in the middle of the circle are neither strongly assertive nor submissive, neither warm nor cold-hearted. The way that they interact with other characters is less clearly interpreted and while for some characters this could be read as intriguing and mysterious, there is also the danger that interactions with these characters may, instead, come across as simply bland.

Let's take a look at how the Interpersonal Circumplex can be applied to understand the relationship styles of some of the main characters in *A Song of Ice and Fire* (1996–) and its television adaptation *Game of Thrones* (2011–18). I've plotted the variety of interpersonal styles that we see in the series in Figure 7.2.

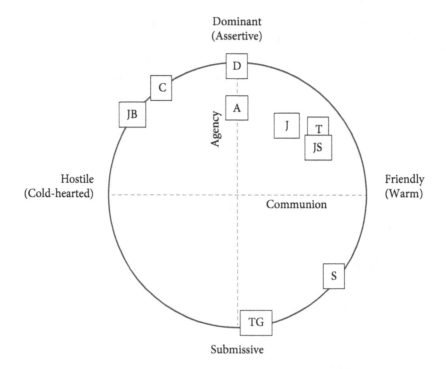

KEY

A=Arya Stark; B=Bran Stark; C=Cersei Lannister; D=Daenerys Targaryen; J=Jaime; JB=Joffrey Baratheon; JS=Jon Snow; S=Samwell Tarly; TG=Theon Greyjoy; T=Tyrion Lannister

Figure 7.2 Interpersonal Circumplex for *Game of Thrones* characters.

In the same way that context plays an important role in shaping our behaviour, context is also important in the way that characters express their interpersonal styles. Although Cersei Lannister is usually cold-hearted and dominant, she is generally warmer in her relationship with her lover/brother Jaime and their son Joffrey. In Figure 7.2, I've placed Cersei (C) and Joffrey in the top left quadrant of the Circumplex and along its circumference, since they are both arrogant, calculating, cold-hearted and dominant characters. Cersei's brothers Jaime (JL) and Tyrion Lannister (T) are also dominant, but more gregarious, so I've placed them in the top right quadrant, along with Jon Snow (JS). Daenerys Targaryen (D) is highly agentic, and depending on the context varies between acting in extremely hostile and cold-hearted ways with others and being somewhat friendly, so I've placed her at the top of the Circumplex. Arya Stark (A) is also dominant, though far less so than Daenerys, and sits somewhere in the middle between warm and cold-hearted. Finally, in the bottom right quadrant, I've placed friendly and submissive Samwell Tarly (S) as well as Theon Greyjoy (TG), who has an interesting arc which takes him from arrogant and assertive to submissive, where I place him now.

What's interesting to note when looking at Figure 7.2 are the wide range of interpersonal styles that we see across the primary and secondary characters of *A Song of Ice and Fire*. And, of course, there are many additional characters in the series whom I haven't plotted here. The strong agentic types are needed to create the conflict and race for power in the narrative, while the more submissive characters, like Samwell Tarly and Theon Greyjoy, are needed as counterpoints. Similarly, while several of the key characters in the series including Cersei and her son Joffrey are truly cold-hearted, others including Samwell Tarly, Jon Snow and Tyrion balance their icy ways with warmth and compassion.

Most longer-form stories need the balance that comes with a variety of characters whose interpersonal styles fall across all four quadrants of the Circumplex. Within these quadrants, characters who are in the top right quadrant will generally be the most appealing. Friendly and dominant, they are likely to have the closest friendships with other characters, and would typically be most attractive as partners. By contrast, the deepest conflict is generated by characters who are hostile and dominant and fall in the top left quadrant. Characters who fall in the bottom right quadrant remind us of our need for connection and cooperation with others and are often essential foils to more dominant characters.

The functions of secondary characters

From the moment we're born we start taking on different roles in life – from daughter or son to friend, colleague, parent and mentor, mirroring similar functions that characters perform in fiction. Let's take a look at what psychological research can tell us about friendships, romantic relationships, family relationships and antagonists that may be useful in creating more believable characters.

Friends

For most of us and our characters alike, our friendships help remind us of who we are. They provide us with companionship, support, compassion and advice. They provide a sounding board for new ideas and they help steer our choices. At times they are also a source of conflict. So, who do we typically choose as a friend and why? One study by psychologists found that people generally tend to select friends who are similarly agreeable, extrovert and open to experience as themselves.[4] Openness to experience is important in friendship because it influences our beliefs, as well as the things that we like to do, and the subjects that we enjoy talking about. Unsurprisingly, extroverts and more agreeable people tend to make the most number of friends. Introverts, however, typically have deeper relationships. They make less friends, but they are more likely to understand these friends' needs, and share more intimacies with them. Of all qualities, neuroticism is the most toxic in friendships.[5]

As writers, we are probably as interested in what creates conflict between our characters and drives them apart as we are in what brings them together. These differences between our characters are essential in creating conflict, driving the story forwards and facilitating the protagonist's growth. Thinking about the main characters in the American buddy movie *Sideways* (2004), for example, Miles is a pessimistic introvert, who is moderately disagreeable, neurotic, conscientious and somewhat open to experience. On the Interpersonal Circumplex he'd fall somewhere in the lower left quadrant. By contrast his buddy Jack is a highly optimistic extrovert, who is agreeable, emotionally stable, unconscientious and open to experience. He'd take a place on the upper right quadrant of the Interpersonal Circumplex. What Miles and Jack have in common is their history as college roommates, a mutual love of wine and an interest in the arts and culture – Miles is a writer and Jack is a former actor. Their differences on every other dimension of their personalities create the conflict that is at the heart of this comedy. While Jack views his final week of unmarried life as the chance to have a few more flings, Miles is unimpressed by his lack of commitment towards his fiancée and Jack's lies that go with it. Meanwhile Miles' disposition towards depression and anxiety irritates the far more emotionally stable Jack, particularly when Miles doesn't manage to keep these feelings under check during what would have otherwise been a fun double date. These differences between their personalities help force Miles to reflect on what's really important to him. Through Jack's more gregarious ways, Miles meets his new love interest Maya which allows him to move on from his past.

Table 7.1 Contrasting Big Five personality dimensions for Miles and Jack from *Sideways* (2004)

	Miles	Jack
Extroversion	Low	High
Agreeableness	Moderate	High
Neuroticism	Moderate/High	Low
Conscientiousness	Moderate	Low
Openness	Moderate	High

Love interest

Some of the most memorable fictional relationships are between characters who fall in love, from Elizabeth Bennet and Mr Darcy in *Pride and Prejudice* (Austen, 1813), through Rick and Isla in *Casablanca* (1942), Jack Twist and Ennis Del Mar in *Brokeback Mountain* (2005) to Beth and Randall in *This is Us* (2016–). What can psychology tell us about creating this kind of magic? This is the point at which I'd love to be able to share a robust and cross-culturally tested formula that gives you the precise ingredients to spark chemistry between your characters. But, of course, if any psychologist really understood what's behind human attraction, chances are they'd be the billionaires behind a new dating agency and you'd already know everything there is to know about their theories. What psychologists have learnt is that people's preferences in partners differ depending on whether they're looking for a short- or longer-term relationship. Unsurprisingly, for short-term sexual relationships men and women place greater emphasis on their partner's physical attractiveness. In terms of personality, agreeableness and extroversion appear to be universally appealing.[6] People are generally more attracted to others whom they see as similar to themselves in relation to their agency and communion. So, individuals who are high in agency tend to prefer attractiveness and status in their partner, while people who are high in communion usually seek out warmer and more caring dates.[7] If in real life we tend to be more attracted to people who are more similar to us in terms of our agency and communion, is this also what we typically see in some of the best loved fictional couples? Let's take a look at a couple of examples to find out.

Scarlett O'Hara and Rhett Butler

Close to the top of many lists of the most popular movie couples of all time are Scarlett O'Hara and Rhett Butler from *Gone with the Wind* (1939), adapted from the 1936 novel of the same name. For Scarlett and Rhett, is theirs a case of opposites attract or are they actually very similar? Let's take a look at how they would rate on the Big Five personality dimensions as illustrated in Table 7.2.

Table 7.2 Contrasting Big Five personality dimensions for Scarlett O'Hara and Rhett Butler from *Gone with the Wind* (1939)

	Scarlett	Rhett
Extroversion	High	Moderate/High
Agreeableness	Low	Low
Neuroticism	High	Low
Conscientiousness	Low	Moderate
Openness	Low	High

Like Scarlett, Rhett is a highly agentic character. He's an alpha male, driven by desires for wealth and freedom, while Scarlett is on the make. As research predicts, they appear to be drawn to each other because they both value agency, attractiveness and status over warmth and agreeableness. Despite this, what's interesting about their characters and essential for their passion is the fact that they are both tender-minded, a facet more typically associated with characters who are highly agreeable. Together with the impulsive, assertive and disagreeable side of their natures, this tender-mindedness sparks their passion. Love and relationships really matter to Scarlett and Rhett. In addition, Rhett is shown to be the only person to understand what makes Scarlett tick, because in many ways they're similar. In Rhett's own words taken from the novel *For I do love you, Scarlett, because we are so much alike, renegades, both of us, dear, and selfish rascals.*

Where the couple differ is on emotional stability and openness to experience. While Scarlett is hot-headed and prone to emotional ups and downs, one of the reasons that Rhett seems to be good for her is that he's much more emotionally stable. He's also more open to experience, which helps open Scarlett's outlook on life. As a fictional couple, Scarlett and Rhett work because of their similarities, which draw them together and allow them to share a somewhat similar world view, as well as their differences which create a complement between their personalities.

Carol and Therese

Compared with Scarlett and Rhett, the characters of Carol and Therese from the critically applauded drama film *Carol* (2015) and the novel from which it was adapted, *The Price of Salt* (Highsmith, 1952), reveal a very different kind of on-screen chemistry that fits perfectly with this story of longing and loss. In the film, and also in the original novel on which it was based, Therese is portrayed as a curious enigma to the far more confident, active, assertive and outgoing Carol. To Carol, Therese's introversion, and the other ways in which she differs from her, make her intriguing. There is also the suggestion that Therese needs to be with someone more confident and extrovert in order to reveal herself. Another dimension on which Carol and Therese differ is their conscientiousness. While the main conflict for Carol comes from the possibility of being separated from her daughter should her affair with Therese break up her marriage, Therese, by contrast, is depicted as having intentionally severed her relationship with her mother. So, while Carol is portrayed as conscientious and bound by loyalty to her family, Therese appears to find it easier to move on from relationships.

What Carol and Therese have in common is their openness to experience. In the novel Therese is portrayed as working as a set designer, who loves the

Table 7.3 Contrasting Big Five personality dimensions for Carol and Therese from *Carol* (2015)

	Carol	Therese
Extroversion	Moderate	Low
Agreeableness	Moderate	Moderate
Neuroticism	Low	Moderate
Conscientiousness	High	Moderate
Openness to experience	Moderate	High

theatre, poetry, travel and exploring a variety of emotional experiences. Carol is also shown to love travel and appreciate aesthetics. From the level of interest that she shows in the details of Therese's life, we can surmise that she is interested in and appreciates their differences. Their chemistry is sparked by this desire to better know and understand each other. It is the longing of two tender-minded people in love, who we sense would perfectly complement each other, but who are separated by the different lives they have chosen as well as the cultural and legal barriers at the time.

Long-term romantic partnerships

When it comes to long-term romantic partnerships, there are far clearer patterns of what works, and what tends not to work. Couples who are opposites in terms of their emotional stability and extroversion, but more similar in their levels of conscientiousness, agreeableness and openness are more likely to stay together.[8] Interestingly, although partnerships between extroverts and introverts are often complementary, research suggests this is sometimes to the detriment of the more introverted partner. This may be because highly extroverted people are more likely to meet and form relationships with other potential partners which are viewed as threatening.[9] Another personality factor that contributes towards the breakdown of relationships is high neuroticism. Toxic relationships are often due to one or both partners scoring high on this factor.[10]

Enough with the research – let's take a look at how these personality factors contribute towards the breakdown of the fictitious relationship between central characters Joan Archer and Joe Castleman in the US drama film *The Wife* (2017), based on the novel of the same name.

Joan Archer and Joe Castleman

Initially attracted by Professor Joe Castleman's confidence, gregariousness and charm, it is these qualities associated with extroversion, alongside their mutual love for literature, that appeal to his far more introverted student Joan Archer, and which, along with their mutual love of literature, appear to have sustained their marriage for many years. Joe enjoys the limelight and understands how to get people's attention with the subject of his stories, while tender-minded and introverted Joan experiences relationships more deeply and knows how to write. She also recognizes how difficult it is to make a living as a female writer, particularly with her quieter personality. In the early years of their relationship,

Table 7.4 Contrasting Big Five personality dimensions for Joan and Joe Castleman from *The Wife* (2017)

	Joan	Joe
Extroversion	Low	High
Agreeableness	Moderate	Moderate
Neuroticism	Moderate	Low
Conscientiousness	High	Moderate
Openness to experience	High	High

they enjoy the complementary attributes that sustain Joan's vision of what a writer must be.

Table 7.4 illustrates how Joan and Joe are complementary in their levels of extroversion and emotional stability, but more similar in conscientiousness, agreeableness and openness to experience – qualities that research suggests should sustain their relationship. And perhaps these qualities would have sustained their relationship if they hadn't entered into a duplicitous arrangement through which Joe takes credit for Joan's writing. Joe's lower conscientiousness and higher extroversion ultimately tear their marriage apart. Joan grows resentful that Joseph has taken all the credit for her writing over the previous thirty years. Not only that, he's also been having affairs. With their relationship reaching a crisis point when Joe wins a Nobel Prize, Joan can no longer bear the strain. Reflecting the research findings on which personality dimensions typically sustain a long-term relationship, and which are most likely to destroy it, the way in which Joe and Joan's relationship is depicted in *The Wife* appears to hold a mirror to the way certain relationships unfold in real life.

Family members

Moving on from romantic relationships, if you are creating characters within the same family, you may be wondering how similar they should be. From your own experience you're bound to know family members who are very similar, as well as others who you'd never guess are related. So how important is nature compared with nurture? And if family members are very different, how do we make it plausible that they are genetically connected? In terms of personality, twin studies demonstrate that our genetics play the most important role in our inheriting openness to experience, followed by extroversion, conscientiousness

Table 7.5 Contrasting Big Five personality dimensions for Tyrion, Cersei and Jaime Lannister from *A Song of Ice and Fire* (1996–)

	Tyrion	Cersei	Jaime
Extroversion	High	Moderate	High
Agreeableness	Moderate	Low	Moderate
Neuroticism	Moderate	Moderate	Moderate
Conscientiousness	High	High	Moderate
Openness	High	Moderate	Moderate

and neuroticism.[11,12] This means that genetically related family members are most likely to rate similarly on openness to experience, but there is still a lot of variability that is accounted for by environmental factors – including, but not limited to, the way that we are brought up.

Thinking about this in relation to the three best-known members of the Lannister family in *A Song of Ice and Fire* / *Game of Thrones* (2011–19), it is evident that siblings Cersei, Jaime and Tyrion share clear similarities as well as differences. To some degree they are all extroverts, but they differ in terms of the facets on which they rate most highly. Cersei is the most assertive, Tyrion the most gregarious, and Jaime is drawn towards seeking excitement. All three are moderately emotionally stable, but again differ in the specific qualities that show this. Cersei and Tyrion share a vulnerability, while Cersei and Jaime are the most impulsive. Cersei alone scores moderately high on anger hostility. Of the three siblings, Tyrion is by far the most agreeable and the most likely to be straightforward, modest and tender-minded. At the other end of the spectrum, Cersei is selfish, manipulative, untrusting, competitive, immodest and cold-hearted. The Lannister siblings are more similar in their levels of conscientiousness and openness to experience as we see in Table 7.5.

So what conclusions can we draw from this? The similarities between these fictional siblings are strong enough for us to believe in their common heritage. But it is the differences between these characters – particularly on certain highly expressed facets of personality – that are most dramatically interesting and provide conflict.

Antagonists

As we saw in Chapter 2, antagonistic characters score high on the attributes of the *Dark Triad* of personality. They're typically narcissistic, Machiavellian and

Table 7.6 Contrasting Dark Triad ratings for Abigail Hall, Queen Anne and the Duchess of Marlborough from *The Favourite* (2018)

	Machiavellianism	Narcissism	Psychopathy
Abigail Hall	High	Moderate	Moderate
Queen Anne	Low	High	Low
Duchess of Marlborough	High	Moderate	Moderate

somewhat psychopathic. The greater the stakes of your film or novel, the higher we'd expect to see the antagonist rate on these traits. So, while a world-saving, high-on-the-Light-Triad Marvel superhero will typically be pitted against an insanely egotistical, scheming, cruel and callous villain, such extremes would be completely over the top and unbelievable in the antagonist of low-key drama. In more realistic fiction, we expect to encounter antagonistic characters with lower ratings on the Dark Triad and who will have both good and bad qualities. In many narratives, the greatest antagonistic forces aren't external but lie within the main character. If we take the British Academy Award-winning historical drama *The Favourite* (2018), for example, there are dark traits in each of the three main characters, as illustrated in Table 7.6. It is precisely these traits that make the three main characters and their interactions with each other so fascinating.

How different characters get what they want

Different characters have not only different motivations but also different styles of trying to get the things that they want. So what are these different styles and which kinds of people are most likely to use them? Psychologists have found that there are an astonishing twelve different ways in which we try to manipulate others. These are *charm, reason, coercion,* the *silent treatment, debasement, regression, appealing to responsibilities, reciprocity, bribes, emphasising the pleasure to be had, social comparison* and by *using hardball tactics.* The methods that we use to try and achieve our goals tell us a lot about our personalities as we'll see in the pages that follow. Let's look at each of these methods in turn along with some examples of the characters who use them.

The Science of Writing Characters

Charm

We're all familiar with the ways in which people charm others into getting what they want. Charm may involve giving personal compliments, being romantic, proffering gifts or even volunteering favours. It is more frequently used to get people to do something, rather than stopping them from doing something and unsurprisingly tends to be used more in romantic relationships than with friends or parents. Let's take a look at an example of the way that Dr Hannibal Lecter uses charm in a brief excerpt from the screenplay for *The Silence of the Lambs* (1991).

>   DR LECTER
>   You're very frank, Clarice. I think
>   it would be quite something to know
>   you in your private life.

Source: Excerpt from unknown draft screenplay for *The Silence of the Lambs* (1991). Written by Ted Tally. Based on the novel by Thomas Harris. Courtesy: Strong Heart/Demme Production and Orion Pictures.

Spoken by someone else, these flattering and very personal lines might be welcome, but when voiced by one of the most well-known and brilliant psychopaths from twentieth-century fiction, they are creepy and disturbing. Dr Lecter's goal here is to provoke Clarice, so that he can enjoy her reactions.

Appealing to responsibilities

Another way in which people try to get what they want is by appealing to responsibility, in other words, by making the case that something needs to be done by someone because it is that person's duty to do it, and they have taken on a commitment to do this. For example, in the following excerpt from American crime film *Goodfellas* (1990), Karen tells her husband that she doesn't want to go on living a life of crime. As she appeals to him with her reminder that she has a duty to her family, she tries to get her way by implicitly reminding him that he also has responsibilities towards her.

>   KAREN
>   I'm not going to run. Live the rest
>   of our lives like rats. Is

```
that what you want? Leave my
mother. Leave my family. Never
see anybody again.
```

Source: Excerpt from shooting draft (January 3, 1989) for *Goodfellas* (1990). Written by Nicholas Pileggi and Martin Scorsese. Courtesy: Warner Bros.

Appealing to reason

Appeals to reason, a technique used more frequently by people who are highly conscientious, remind us of why we should do something. This could involve pointing out the good things that will come from that action, or explaining why someone is making that appeal. In the following excerpt from the pilot for the British TV series *Killing Eve* (2018–), Eve appeals to reason when her first request to be present in a witness interview is refused. When she isn't successful, she asserts she's going to do it anyway.

```
                    EVE
        Would you mind if I asked to be
        present in the witness interview?

                    BILL
        Sure, if you're an agent. But
        you're a glorified security guard
        so.. Dang sorry.

                    EVE
        But if it's a new assassin, we need to
        know as much as we can as soon as we -

                    BILL
        Yes I would mind. Your time is
        mine. I own you.

                    EVE
        I'm going to do it anyway.
```

Source: Excerpt from shooting script for the pilot of *Killing Eve* (2018). Written by Phoebe Waller-Bridge. Courtesy: Sid Gentle Films for BBC America.

Emphasizing the pleasure to be had

For agreeable people, who are sensitive to other people's needs and prefer to be cooperative rather than demanding, getting people to do what they want has to be done in the most pleasant way possible. In order to do this they usually emphasize the pleasure to be had. For example, in a romantic scene in the American comedy-drama *Sideways* (2004), when the protagonist's love interest, Maya, wants to persuade him to open a special bottle of wine that he was saving, here's the way that she phrases it and makes her claim hard to resist:

```
                    MAYA
     The day you open a '61 Cheval Blanc,
     that's the special occasion.
```

Source: Excerpt from May 29, 2003 script for *Sideways* (2004). Written by Alexander Payne and Jim Taylor. Courtesy: Michael London Productions.

Reciprocity

Appealing to reciprocity is about proposing a reward or favour in return for someone doing something for you. In other words: 'If you help me, I'll help you.' In the following excerpt from the screenplay for the pilot episode of the TV series *Breaking Bad* (2008–13), Walter White is threatened with a gun by a rival dealer. He offers to demonstrate how to cook his special meth recipe in exchange for being allowed to keep his life.

```
                    WALT
     W-What if I showed you my secret? Every
     cook's got his recipe -- what if I
     taught you mine?
                (off their silence)
     Let us both live, I'll teach you.
```

Source: Excerpt from May 27, 2005 script for the pilot episode of *Breaking Bad* (2008). Written by Vince Gilligan. Courtesy: AMC / Sony Pictures Television.

Social comparison

Individuals who are more closed to experience often use social comparison when trying to get their own way. They might make a preferential comparison to someone else who would perform their desired activity. Or they might insist that they would look stupid if they didn't do it. In the following excerpt from teen comedy *Mean Girls* (2004), when Cady tells 'Queen Bee' Regina that she plans on joining the Mathletes, Regina gets her own way by using the following social comparison:

>   REGINA
> No, no, no. You cannot do that. That is
> social suicide. Damn, you are so lucky you
> have us to guide you.

Source: Excerpt from June 3, 2003 script for *Mean Girls* (2004). Written by Tina Fey. Courtesy of Paramount Pictures / M.G. Films / Broadway Video.

Debasement

People who use debasement to get what they want will typically put themselves down, lower themselves or act humble. In the following excerpt from one of the final scenes in the historical drama *Schindler's List* (1993), Schindler puts down his efforts to save the Jews in an attempt to stop Stern from congratulating him. He feels he should have saved more people from their deaths and won't hear otherwise.

>   SCHINDLER
> If I'd made more money ... I threw away
> so much money, you have no idea. If I'd
> just ...
>
>   STERN
> There will be generations because of
> what you did.
>
>   SCHINDLER
> I didn't do enough.

Source: Excerpt from (March 1990) first revision script for *Schindler's List* (1993). Written by Steven Zallian. Courtesy: Universal Pictures / Amblin Entertainment.

Coercion

Coercive people use demands or threats to get someone to do what they want. They may force people to do something, criticize them, threaten or shout at them until they perform that action. Coercion has been found to be most commonly used by people who are highly disagreeable or neurotic, as well as by male extroverts, when trying to get friends or partners to stop doing something.[13] In the following excerpt from the American drama *Gran Torino* (2008), the character played by Clint Eastwood threatens local kids in his front garden that if they don't leave, he'll respond with violence.

> WALT
>
> Don't think for a second I won't blow a
> big hole in your face and it won't bother
> me a bit, not any more than if I shot a
> deer. Now get off my goddamned lawn.

Source: Excerpt from unknown draft script for *Gran Torino* (2008). Written by Nick Schenk. Courtesy: Double Nickel Entertainment / Malpaso Productions / Village Roadshow Pictures.

Regression

Regression involves whining or sulking until you get what you want and is most commonly used by people who are high on neuroticism. Here's an excerpt from *Gone with the Wind* (1939) in which Scarlett O' Hara uses her practised expertise in this technique in order to get her friends to stop talking about war:

> SCARLETT
>
> Fiddle-dee-dee! War, war, war! This war
> talk's spoiling all the fun at every
> party this Spring! I get so bored I
> could scream!

> She makes a motion to indicate in affected fashion just
> how annoyed she is by this boring subject.

Source: Excerpt from unknown draft script for *Gone with the Wind* (1939). Written by Sidney Howard. Based on the novel by Margaret Mitchell. Courtesy: Turner Entertainment Co and O.S.P. Publishing Inc.

Bribes

Offering a monetary reward in exchange for doing something is a tactic most commonly used by people who are higher on neuroticism. But like all these strategies, it isn't confined to just one personality type. Here is an excerpt from the screenplay for *The Wolf of Wall Street* (2013) in which Jordan Belfort offers an FBI agent a bribe.

JORDAN
See, it's all about proper guidance,
Pat. Knowing someone with the right
relationships, who's discreet. I can
change a life almost every day.

They measure each other.

AGENT DENHAM
How much that intern make off your deal?

JORDAN

North of half a million.

Denham summons agent Hughes over. To Denham:

AGENT DENHAM
Can you say that again, what you told me?
(Jordan declines with a smile;
to Agent Hughes)

I believe Mr Belfort just tried to bribe a
federal officer.

Source: Excerpt from (March 5, 2013) shooting script for *The Wolf of Wall Street* (2013). Written by Terence Winter. Courtesy: Red Granite Pictures / Appian Way / Sikelia Productions / EMJAG Productions.

Hardball tactics

Hardball tactics involve lying, threatening or using violence, threatening to leave someone, degrading someone, or withholding money until someone does what's being asked of them. Following is an example from the American drama *Whiplash* (2014), when antagonistic music teacher Fletcher uses violence to try to get his student Andrew to slow down his rhythm on the drums.

```
Andrew nods. Get it together ... Fletcher claps.
Stops.

                    FLETCHER (CONT'D)
                 You're rushing.

Claps again. Stops again.

                    FLETCHER (CONT'D)
                   Dragging.

Claps again. Andrew plays WHIPLASH STUDIO BAND
REHEARSAL ANDREW #3, expecting another stop -- but it
doesn't come. Fletcher nods, as though now satisfied,
then slowly turns around. Puts his hand on a spare
chair. Looks like he's about to sit down, when ...

... like a flash of lightning he WHIPS up the chair and
HURLS it straight at Andrew's head.
```

Source: Excerpt from shooting script for *Whiplash* (2014). Written by Damien Chazelle. Courtesy: Bold Films / Blumhouse Productions / Right of Way Films / Sierra / Infinity.

The power of silence

The emotional impact of being ostracized or being given the silent treatment can be very powerful because, as we've seen, belonging is a fundamental and universal human need. When people are ostracized, excluded or rejected it can have dire effects on their mental health.[14] Giving someone the silent treatment is most frequently used as a form of punishment, in order to get someone to stop doing something.[15] It can also be used by a group as a way of making an example of someone who has done something that they consider to be shameful. In the American historical novel *The Scarlet Letter* (Hawthorner, 1850), protagonist Hester Prynne is ostracized by her Puritan community after having a child with another man, while she was married. And in the example that follows, the main character in the romantic drama *Revolutionary Road* (2008) uses silence to express the distance she's now feeling from her husband as their lives grow apart.

                         FRANK
          I don't think I suggested we talk about
          everything all the time. My point was,
          we've both been under a strain and we
          ought to be trying to help each other
          as much as we can right now.

She's utterly uninterested and it's making him nervous.

                         FRANK (CONT'D)
          I mean God knows my own behavior has
          been pretty weird lately... I mean,
          as it happens... there is actually
          something I'd like to tell you about...

She continues folding the napkins.

                         FRANK (CONT'D)
          I've been with a girl in the city a few
          times.

Finally, she stops moving. She looks at him.

                         FRANK (CONT'D)
          A girl I hardly even know. It was
          nothing to me, but she got a little
          carried away. She's just a kid...
          Anyway, it's over now. It's really
          over. If I weren't sure of that I guess
          I could never have told you

about it.

Source: Excerpt from the first draft script for *Revolutionary Road* (2008). Written by Justin Haythe. Courtesy: DreamWorks / BBC Films / Evamere Entertainment /Neal Street Productions / Goldcrest Pictures and Scott Rudin Productions.

When April finally responds, it is simply to ask Frank why he had to tell her about this. For April, silence is her way of coping with a situation that she is profoundly unhappy about. It's her way of retreating into herself and communicating that she doesn't have the energy to continue like this. While April uses silence to try and get what she wants, Frank tries to reason with her and suggests that they have a more reciprocal relationship from now on. It's a useful reminder that characters with different motivations and different personalities typically use different techniques to try and get what they want. The interplay between these different strategies can be fascinating.

Drawing it all together

Secondary characters breathe additional life into our stories. They help drive the narrative forwards, force the protagonist to make interesting choices and reveal other truths about our human nature. They also contribute towards the tone of the narrative as well its style and pace. When thinking about secondary characters, you'll first need to decide what kind of characters you'll require – for example, friends, colleagues, family members and antagonists – and then who each of these characters are. As you begin to consider how much story time you'll spend with each of these characters, you'll have a better understanding of the complexities with which you'll need to write them. While some of your secondary characters may need to be shown in action across all five dimensions and multiple facets of personality, those with which we spend the least time may be sufficiently captured on just two or three dimensions.

Having understood who your characters are, next it's time to start thinking about their relationships. Although similarities between some characters' personalities may help to bring them together, differences are vital for creating conflict and variety. Similarities and differences in characters' relationship styles can be visualized on the Interpersonal Circumplex and this is a useful way of ensuring that you have the variety of interpersonal styles that are needed by most longer-form narratives. Remember also that relationships are dynamic,

Table 7.7 How personality influences the way in which people try to get what they want

	With friends	**With partners**	**With parents**
Extrovert	Appeal to responsibilities; men also use coercion	Men use coercion	Appeal to responsibilities with fathers
Introvert		Debasement	Hardball tactics and debasement, the latter particularly with mothers
Agreeable	Emphasize the pleasure to be had	Emphasize the pleasure to be had and use reason	Emphasize the pleasure to be had
Disagreeable		Coercion and the silent treatment	
Conscientious	Reason	Reason	
Unconscientious			
Neurotic		Regression, coercion and financial reward	
Emotionally stable		Hardball tactics and reason	
Open to experience	Reason and emphasize the pleasure to be had	Reason and emphasize the pleasure to be had	Reason and emphasize the pleasure to be had
Closed to experience	Social comparison	Social comparison	Social comparison

Source: Buss, David M. 'Manipulation in close relationships: Five personality factors in interactional context.' *Journal of Personality* (1992)

and most interesting when we portray them in flux. Your characters will bring their own goals, beliefs and moods to each of their relationships. Charting the highs and lows of your characters' relationships as you plan your story will help keep your story alive and your readers engaged. For each scene in which your characters come together, you'll need to understand what it is that they want and what is the most truthful and interesting way that they can try and achieve this. In any one scene, different characters will be applying different strategies to try and win over each other. Table 7.7 summarizes the main research findings that tell us about how different personality types typically attempt to influence others when trying to achieve their goals.

Having taken a closer look at some of the research-based approaches that may be useful in creating more lifelike and compelling character relationships, in the next chapter we'll be combining these ideas together with all the other approaches that we've discovered in this book in a final character workshop. Take a break, have a coffee and come along!

A character workshop

There is a lot of theory in this book. It's mostly derived from observations of how people act in the real world and how we can usefully apply this knowledge to create more lifelike, engaging and believable characters. But reading theory is a very different process to putting it to use when writing, so this final chapter is designed as a character workshop. It will bring together all the research-based approaches that we've been looking at and help you apply these to whichever characters you are currently developing. Whatever stage you're at in your writing process, there should be something useful for you here. Bring along your first ideas for a completely new character, problems with a character in progress, or character-driven scenes that you're wrestling with and let's workshop these together.

Finding the right protagonist

You might have an idea for a story, a situation that piques your curiosity, or a loose notion of your main character. But how do you go from those first hazy impressions to writing a crystal clear character who comes to life on the page? First, try and bring into focus any of the ideas that you already have. There is a reason why they seem right to you, and these are ideas that you'll probably keep coming back to. Are there certain character traits that you can already see? Or is it obvious to you that your protagonist must have a particular goal? Whatever you have in your mind, jot it down as a valuable starting point and let's take your character forward from here.

Since all fictional characters start with observation from life, whether consciously or unconsciously made, returning to further develop a character from real-life observation is often useful for the next stage of character development. Is there someone who you know, you've seen or heard about who could provide further inspiration for your character? If there is no single person who comes to your mind, could you take interesting traits from a medley of people that you know and combine these to create a new character?

Another way of drawing on observation from life is by casting your main characters. If a film was made from your screenplay or novel, and with budget no obstacle, whom would you cast in the main roles? And what would these actors bring to their roles that you hadn't previously considered? If fantasy-casting doesn't help, how about looking through images of different people's faces online to see if any of those spark ideas for your character or feel right for your story? Since agreeableness and neuroticism can be judged reliably by looking at neutral headshots of the face, and extroversion from full-body posture,[1] using photos of people as visual prompts gives us a lot of information about their personalities that we may not at first be consciously aware of. Creating character mood-boards can also be very useful in the same way. If you've created a character mood-board, spend some time analyzing the faces and postures of the people that you've picked to represent your character. Which aspects of their personalities can you pick up from these? What about the way in which they are dressed, or the mood of the images? Have you chosen images with warmer, brighter colours, and happier faces suggestive of a more agreeable, stable extrovert? Or darker tones, with more serious and anxious faces, which suggest a more neurotic, introverted character?

If you're adapting a character from a work of fiction, a biography, documentary footage or even a newspaper article, you may already have everything that you need to begin writing that character. The source material should give you a good understanding of your main characters' personalities, motivations, beliefs, and even the way that they speak. The choice is then yours about how closely you'll stick with your perceptions. Other starting points for a character may come from a plot or even a theme. You may know that you're writing a detective story in which your investigator needs to track down an international fraudster. So, you know your protagonist's goal, you may have an idea about some of their beliefs, and you'll be able to surmise that they need to be active, assertive, goal-driven and at least somewhat disagreeable in order to get their job done. Next, run through a range of different possibilities to test what works best on their other personality dimensions. For example, would your story work best and have the tone that you envisaged if your protagonist was an emotionally unstable introvert? Or does a chatty, stable, extrovert fit better with the upbeat tone that you had in mind?

Starting with your character's personality

In the first five seconds that we meet a stranger, we make pretty accurate judgements about their levels of extroversion, agreeableness, neuroticism, conscientiousness, negative emotions and even intelligence.[2,3] Starting with extroversion, ask yourself whether your character is more dominant, active and sociable, or someone who is quieter, more serious and needs time on their own? If they're more outgoing, how does this fit with the tone of the genre that you're writing? Does your character need positive emotions because you're writing a warm, upbeat story? Or would a more serious disposition fit better with the darker narrative that you're planning to write? Next, consider whether your character is more agreeable or disagreeable. When we talk about a strong character, we normally mean that they're disagreeable. Characters who speak their own mind and pursue their goals with little concern for others are inherently fascinating and often memorable. On the other hand, more agreeable characters are easier to like, trust and gain our sympathies. We're also more likely to identify with these characters and feel moved by their stories. More agreeable and outgoing protagonists, with more positive emotions, fit better with upbeat narratives, while more disagreeable introverts are more naturally aligned with grittier stories.

Neuroticism is another dimension that we pick up quickly on first impressions. More emotionally unstable protagonists are usually better suited to psychological narratives about internal conflicts, in which your character's main journey may be to overcome their anxiety or self-doubt. High levels of neuroticism are generally less useful in action and adventure genres, in which the protagonist's main journey is external. For these higher-octane narratives, an emotionally stable protagonist is usually a better fit. You may already know whether your character is conscientious. If not, start by thinking about how driven they are to achieve their goal. If you're writing an action, adventure or detective story, it's hard to imagine how any of these would work without having a highly conscientious, achievement-driven protagonist. But there is plenty of scope for less conscientious characters in dramas and comedies.

Finally, how open to experience is your character? Does your story work better if your character embraces adventure, meeting new people, and having a whole variety of new experiences? Or do you create a more interesting story if your character is closed-minded and resistant to the changes that the events of your narrative will force upon them? Once you've decided where your character lies on each of the Big Five dimensions (low, moderate or high), complete Table 8.1.

Table 8.1 Rate your character on the Big Five dimensions

	Extroversion	Agreeableness	Neuroticism	Conscientiousness	Openness
Low					
Moderate					
High					

Remember that characters who score moderately across all five dimensions will typically be less memorable. So in order to create a memorable central character, make sure that they rate towards the extremes of at least one or two of these dimensions.

When you later write scenes for your characters with these personality dimensions in mind, remember that these are *dispositions* towards behaving in certain ways, not rule books. Even the most agreeable characters will have moments and situations in which they are disagreeable, just as extroverts will have moments in which they're quieter.

To develop further complexity within your character, it's now time to dive deeper into these personality dimensions and think more closely about how your main character scores on each facet. To create more believable and complex characters, they should score higher on some facets and lower on others within any one personality dimension. So, for example, if you're creating a highly conscientious character who is goal-driven, competent, deliberate and self-disciplined, it could also be interesting to make them disordered in their approach to work. Use Table 8.2 to rate your character on the thirty facets of personality. Only the facets on which your character rates most strongly will create an impression on your readers.

This is a process that is going to take time and may need revisiting over several days or weeks. Finding where your character lies on some of these facets will be harder than others and that may be because they rate more neutrally on these facets. Once you have these ratings, move on to think about how your character

Table 8.2 Rate your character on the thirty facets of personality

Openness	Conscientiousness	Neuroticism	Agreeableness	Extroversion
Fantasy	Competence	Anxiety	Trusting	Warm
Aesthetics	Order	Anger hostility	Straightforward	Gregarious
Feelings	Dutiful	Depression	Altruistic	Assertive
Actions	Achievement-striving	Self-conscious	Compliant	Active
Ideas	Self-discipline	Impulsive	Modest	Excitement-seeking
Values	Deliberation	Vulnerable	Tender-minded	Positive emotions

Table 8.3 Rate your character on the Light Triad

	Kantianism (valuing others for who they are)	Humanism (appreciating others' dignity)	Faith in humanity
Low			
Moderate			
High			

Table 8.4 Rate your character on the Dark Triad

	Machiavellianism (exploitative)	Narcissism (self-important)	Psychopathy (callous & cynical)
Low			
Moderate			
High			

scores on the Light and Dark Triads of personality and complete Tables 8.3 and 8.4. Remember that unless you're intending to create comic book saints and villains, complex characters will have elements of both the Dark and Light Triad.

To help visualize how the Big Five dimensions, the thirty facets of personality, the Light and Dark Triads fit together, take a look at Figure 8.1. In the centre of the circular diagram are the Big Five dimensions of personality. Beyond these, in the second circle, are the thirty facets of personality. The outer circle shows that openness to experience is related to political beliefs, agreeableness is related to the Light and Dark Triads, and neuroticism is related to mental health.

Once you have a better understanding of your main character, next you'll need to think about how to characterize them on the page. Review Chapter 2 to remind yourself of how the Big Five personality dimensions are expressed through action, emotions and interactions with other characters. Finding a voice for your character is such an important part of getting them down on the page that the whole of Chapter 3 was devoted to looking at the relationship between the Big Five personality dimensions and the way that people speak.

Developing your character's voice

The main point to think about when developing a pattern of speech for your character is how they express their personality through their voice. After

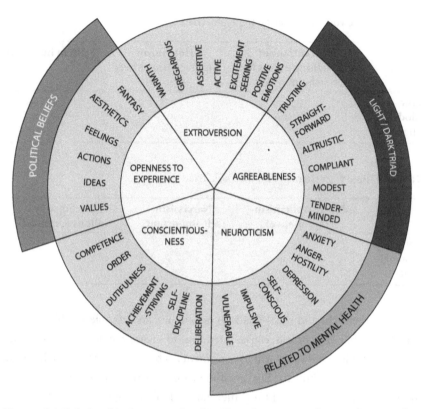

Figure 8.1 Relationship between the Big Five dimensions, facets of personality, political beliefs, mental health and the Light and Dark Triads.
Source: Costa and McCrae, 1992 , Paulhus and Williams, 2002

reviewing Chapter 3, make a note of the dominant dimensions of your character's personality, or in other words, the dimensions on which they score highest or lowest. These are the dimensions that you will need to bring out when writing their dialogue. For example, if your character is highly extrovert and low on agreeableness, but moderate on the three other dimensions, you'll need to ensure that their speech reflects their sociable, chatty, assertive, but disagreeable nature.

Once you've reviewed how your character's personality affects their conversational style, you'll need to connect this theory to your practice as a writer. There are a couple of exercises that may be useful for you here. The first is the widely used dramatic technique known as *hot-seating*. Find some friends or family to be your audience, get into the role of your character, introduce yourself and have your audience ask you questions. The exercise is to respond in character. If your character is a disagreeable extrovert, take the lead in your conversations, be assertive, don't worry about offending those around you and practise using an informal voice. The point of this exercise is to absorb the theory that we've been looking at, step into the role, and find the voice that you'll then be using to write this character.

The second exercise is to try writing a character monologue. Imagine that at the beginning of your story you've asked your character to tell you about their life, and now write this in the first person using their spoken voice. For more extrovert characters, this should be easy as your character would likely talk freely about themselves. For more introvert characters, imagine that they are talking to their closest friend or even a therapist. What would they say? And more importantly, how would they say it? Remember that you'll also need to think about how your character's situation, age, social class and background influence their choice of words. If you're still finding it hard to get down your character's voice, grab a notebook, go out and listen to some real speech. Eavesdrop on conversations between people that sound most like the ones you're writing. Listen to their patterns of speech, the subjects they talk about, and the words they most frequently use. Once you start to get the feel of your character's voice, you'll probably find it that stays. And you might even discover that by finding your character's voice, they start to reveal qualities of their personality that you hadn't previously considered. Run with new ideas during these moments when you're in the flow. This is where your instinct is kicking in.

Giving your character motivations and beliefs

By this stage you'll probably know your character's major motivations. If not, review the twelve evolutionary motivations laid out in Chapter 4 and work out which best fit with your character's journey. If your protagonist transforms, consider whether they start the narrative being motivated by a selfish quest for power and status, and whether they end it being driven by a desire for more connectedness. In addition to thinking about your protagonist's overarching motivation, give some thought to how their initial goal aligns with their beliefs. For example, if your protagonist's initial quest is to earn as much money as possible, this may be because they believe that money brings happiness. If through earning more money your character then finds that happiness doesn't come with it, they will likely reassess their beliefs and find new motivations.

Making your character transform

Continuing to think about how your character transforms, make a note of their motivations at the beginning and then at the end of your narrative in Table 8.5. Then repeat this exercise for their beliefs in Table 8.6. If you're creating a main character whose motivations don't change, skip ahead to the next section and consider whether their beliefs or personality are transformed in any way.

When you've worked out how your protagonist's motivations and beliefs are transformed by the events of the story, next you'll need to work out *what* it is that changes them. What are their peak experiences, low points and turning points, and at what points in the story do these happen? Make a note of these in Table 8.7.

Now that you know which events bring about changes in your protagonist, think about how your character's personality transforms as a result of these experiences. Does the character become more assertive and confident, more agreeable or more open to experience? Jot down these changes in Table 8.8.

Table 8.5 Your protagonist's motivational arc

	Beginning	End
Motivations		

Table 8.6 Your protagonist's changing beliefs

	Beginning	End
Beliefs		

Table 8.7 Your protagonist's turning points, peak experiences and low points

	Beginning	Middle	End
Turning points			
Peak experiences			
Low points			

Table 8.8 Your protagonist's personality change

	Beginning	Middle	End
Personality			

Charting your character's emotional journey

Having worked out the events in your story that help bring about changes in your protagonist, you're already well on your way to knowing their emotional arc. Plot the high and low points of your story on the graph in Figure 8.2. Then think about how your protagonist feels at the beginning of the journey and at its end. Connect these points to chart your main character's emotional journey, then step back and take a look at the graph. Are there enough emotional turning points in your story? If you're aiming to write a page-turner, are the turning points regularly spaced? Are the rising and falling lines between the turning points steep enough to keep your readers engaged? Or if you're creating a slow burning narrative, is the slow increase in tension that you'd envisaged reflected in the arc that you've drawn?

Your main character's range of positive and negative sentiments represent just one dimension of their emotional world. The most engaging characters aren't just happy and sad. Like all of us they experience a wide range of emotions. Use the checklist in Table 8.9 to ensure that your main character has a rich emotional journey.

By this point you should have a pretty good idea of the nuances and complexities of your main character. You'll know what they want as well as what they need. You'll have worked out how they transform, and the

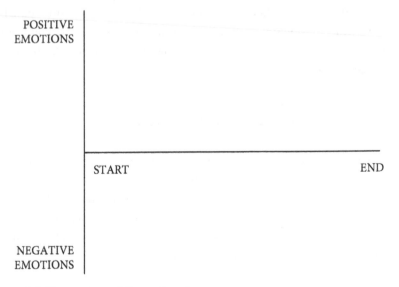

Figure 8.2 Your protagonist's emotional arc.

Table 8.9 Your character's emotional range

Emotion	Example scenes
Anger	
Fear	
Disgust	
Happiness	
Sadness	
Surprise	
Amusement	
Awe	
Contempt	
Contentment	
Desire	
Elevation	
Embarrassment	
Guilt	
Interest	
Jealousy	
Pain	
Pride	
Relief	
Romantic love	
Satisfaction	
Shame	
Sympathy	
Tension	

events of the story that help bring about this change. You'll anticipate how readers will emotionally engage with your protagonist, and you'll know your protagonist's emotional journey. Now it's time to think about your secondary characters.

Creating secondary characters

After you've settled on the roles that secondary characters will be playing in your story, you'll need to start thinking about their personalities. To ensure that you create a good range of characters, with plenty of potential for conflict and personalities that are right for the tone of your story, work through Table 8.10. If you need to add other roles to this chart, or delete character functions that your story doesn't need, go ahead. Then, beginning with your

Table 8.10 Your characters' personalities, beliefs and goals

	Protagonist	Love interest	Friend/other	Antagonist
Extroversion				
Agreeableness				
Neuroticism				
Conscientiousness				
Openness to experience				
Beliefs				
Main goal				

Table 8.11 Your main character's ratings on the Dark and Light Triads

		Protagonist	Love interest	Friend/other	Antagonist
Dark Triad	Machiavellianism				
	Narcissism				
	Psychopathy				
Light Triad	Kantianism				
	Humanism				
	Faith in Humanity				

protagonist, rate the personality dimensions (low, moderate or high) for each of your characters in turn. Think about which dimensions some of your characters score most similarly on, and on which they are polar opposites. Also ensure your characters have different beliefs about the world, which relate to their main goal. With the table complete, take a step back and make sure that it feels right for the story you want to tell. Are any two characters too similar? Is the tone that you'll be setting through this range of characters' personalities right for your story? Don't rush this stage. It will take time, and it's worth getting it right.

Another way of checking that you've created sufficient complexity in your main characters is by checking their scores on the Dark and Light Triads (low, moderate or high). Remember, very few people have entirely good or bad qualities. The vast majority of us are tipped towards the light side, but will also have some traits on the Dark Triad. Antagonists weigh more heavily towards the dark.

Troubleshooting character problems

Hopefully you're now at a point where you've successfully developed characters you can't wait to start writing, but what happens when you run into a problem with their development? You may have a gut instinct that readers aren't going to care about your main character. Or you may have received notes on a first draft telling you that one of your characters needs work. First, know that you're in good company. In my work as a script consultant and screenwriting tutor, there are a number of character-related problems that I see time and time again. Here are some of the problems that I see most frequently, along with my solutions:

PROBLEM: *Your readers don't care about your main character.*
SOLUTIONS: First, think about how you want your readers to feel about your main character. If you're creating a character whom you want your readers to like, then ensure that within the first few minutes of introducing them you give your readers opportunities to like them, trust in them, and believe that they are fundamentally good. Some of the most important attributes that we like in others are captured by the Light Triad and include valuing people for who they are, appreciating their dignity, and believing that people are fundamentally good. Other likeable qualities include warmth, kindness, honesty, a good sense of humour, being cooperative and helpful, and caring about others' feelings. Revealing any of these traits in action will help bring your readers on side.

When creating a more disagreeable main character, who is less instantly likeable, one of the ways in which you can get your audience to care about them is by showing that they are still fundamentally good. You could show that they have a good motivation, or are attempting to do the right thing. Or you could cast your difficult and disagreeable character against more antagonistic and less trustworthy characters. Or you could show that your character has a good reason to be this way, for example, by having had a hard life, while giving them additional qualities that we find redemptive.

Other main characters keep our interest because they are fascinating. They don't have to be likeable, or even particularly sympathetic, but they keep us wanting to know more. If your intention is to create an intriguing main character, then ensure that you give them qualities that keep us second-guessing. They may keep secrets or may be devious, dishonest, impulsive, and emotionally unpredictable. The skill of creating a fascinating character is in making them act in *consistently* unpredictable ways that we find hard to fathom, but still feel believable.

PROBLEM: *Your main character is forgettable and uninteresting.*

SOLUTIONS: There are three main reasons why readers may perceive your main character to be uninteresting and forgettable. The first is by intention, in which case is this what you really want? It is more likely that you've unintentionally written a character who rates moderately across each of the Big Five dimensions, so they fail to make any strong impression. This may be because you've based the character on yourself, and you haven't been sufficiently confident about bringing out any of the more interesting facets of your personality. Another reason is that you may have a great idea for a character in your mind, but struggle to bring them to life on the page. If, for example, you intend your character to be tender-minded and impulsive, but you fail to show this through their actions, thoughts or dialogue, then these characteristics are lost on the reader. Some writers find it useful to create a checklist for their characters' personality traits to ensure that they have them all covered in their writing. Table 8.12 shows an example checklist for a character on the dimension of extroversion. The notes tell us how the writer plans to reveal their character's facets of extroversion within the story and the page numbers tell us where we see these in the story.

Table 8.12 Example of a personality/scene characterization checklist

	Facet	Notes	Pages
Extroversion	Cold	Interactions with others except for oldest friend	2,3,5,7 and so on
	Antisocial	Happiest alone	1,4,6,8 and so on
	Highly assertive	Dominates others in interactions, makes sure she gets what she wants	2,3,5,7 and so on
	Very active	Always on the move and following her plan	1,4,5,6 and so on
	Serious/neutral emotions	Nearly all the time except when joking about with oldest friend	2,3,5,9 and so on
	Seeks excitement	Loves the thrill of danger; rarely considers her own safety	4,9,15 and so on

If you find this approach helps, you can create similar checklists to make sure you've also captured your character's beliefs and motivations on your pages.

PROBLEM: *Readers tell me they don't have a good sense of what my character is like.*

SOLUTIONS: Personality captures the disposition towards behaving in consistent ways. So if you have an idea for a great character, and have created a scene checklist as per the example in Table 8.12 to ensure you are revealing these personality traits on the page, but still get feedback from readers telling you that they don't have a strong idea of who your character is, it may be that your character isn't acting consistently enough to give readers the sense that they have a strong core to their personalities. For example, if your character saves a cat once, but at other times ignores cats in peril or actively endangers cats, we're more likely to conclude that your character is emotionally unstable rather than that they are a tender-minded animal lover. To clearly communicate your character's personality within your story, you have to ensure that their personality traits aren't revealed just once or twice, but consistently throughout the story. This doesn't mean that your highly disagreeable character should be grumpy and argumentative at every moment that we see them, because the expression of personality traits is dependent on context, but that most of the time they act in disagreeable ways. In a few well-chosen situations, for example, when sharing a proud moment with someone they love, they may be agreeable. It is this consistency with which personality traits are revealed, along with the less frequent context-dependent moments that we see characters act in counter-dispositional ways, which allows readers to know who your characters are and to believe in them.

PROBLEM: *All your characters' dialogues sound the same.*

SOLUTIONS: Review Chapter 3 on dialogue, write a monologue for each of your main characters and get to know their voices before starting your rewrite. Remember that extrovert characters tend to be talkative, flit from subject to subject and speak in an informal manner. Introverts talk less and stay on one topic only. Agreeable characters are sympathetic, cooperative and positive; they're also mostly concerned with making sure that the characters they're speaking to feel comfortable. Disagreeable characters are blunt, direct and say what they think. Characters who score higher on neuroticism tend to be more negative and talk more about themselves. Emotionally stable characters are calm and comfortable in conversation. Characters who are more open to experience love debate and use rich language, while characters who are closed to experience tend to use more simple language. You don't need to capture your character's personality on all five dimensions in the way that they speak – instead, find a way of expressing them on the two or three dimensions that they rate most extremely on. If you're still struggling to get this down on the page, then eavesdrop on some real-world conversations between people who are most similar to your characters, make some notes and use these to inform your characters' speech. Always remember to read your dialogue aloud.

PROBLEM: *Your story is missing drama.*
SOLUTIONS: Lack of drama in a story may mean that there isn't enough conflict between your characters. It could also mean that your main character doesn't face enough obstacles, or that they don't appear to have any internal conflict. To solve these problems, ensure that you pit your protagonist against more antagonistic characters who score higher on the Dark Triad and whose motivations, opposing values and beliefs conflict with those of your protagonist. One way of giving your characters opposing beliefs is by placing them at the opposite ends of the spectrum on openness to experience. Characters who are more open are typically more liberal in their world view, while characters who are more closed are more conservative. In addition to ramping up interpersonal conflict between your characters you may also need to give your main character more external obstacles. These will contribute towards the life events that form the peaks and troughs of their emotional journey. It is also important to remember that without high points in your main character's emotional journey, we won't appreciate their low points. Drama comes from the excitement that we experience as a story swings between moments in which things go well for the protagonist to the moments in which their fortunes change.

Some final words

I need to make a confession at this point. Writers who come along to my workshops often tell me the same thing as we finish: they need a coffee. I tend to cover a lot of ground and I cover it fast. If you've attempted to read this book in one or two sittings then you may well be feeling overwhelmed by theory.

Hopefully, after a day or two, the big ideas here will start to stick and in time they may become part of the regular way in which you develop new characters. What I hope to have achieved in this book is an account of psychological research and theory that questions, explains and elaborates upon some of the main ideas that are taught about writing characters. For example, how we can make characters that are rounded and complex, why and how characters typically transform, and how we can create more emotionally engaging characters. You may find that the framework proposed in this book is immediately helpful in creating new characters from the ground up. Or you may come to discover that you prefer to work from instinct on your first draft, and then use particular approaches to review how well your characters are working, and fix any problems that you might find. There is no right way to write. Find the way that works best for you. There is, however, only one way to develop great characters, and that is through combining your imagination with your observations from life. Our characters come from our experiences of life, and it is only by studying life that we'll write the best stories. We just need to open our eyes, our hearts and our minds.

Notes

Chapter 1

1 Raymond Federman, 'Surfiction: A postmodern position', in *Moderne Erzähltheorie* (Stuttgart: UTB, 1993), 413–29.

2 Edward Morgan Forster, *Aspects of the Novel*, vol. 19 (Boston: Houghton Mifflin Harcourt, 1985).

3 David M. Buss, 'Evolutionary psychology: A new paradigm for psychological science', *Psychological Inquiry* 6, no. 1 (1995): 1–30.

4 David Sloan Wilson, 'Evolutionary social constructivism', in *The Literary Animal: Evolution and the Nature of Narrative*, ed. Jonathan Gottschall and David Sloan Wilson (Evanston: Northwestern University Press, 2005), 20–9.

5 Kate C. McLean, Monisha Pasupathi and Jennifer L. Pals, 'Selves creating stories creating selves: A process model of self-development', *Personality and Social Psychology Review* 11, no. 3 (2007): 262–78.

Chapter 2

1 Ernest C. Tupes and Raymond E. Christal, 'Recurrent personality factors based on trait ratings', *Journal of Personality* 60, no. 2 (1992): 225–51.

2 Robert R. McCrae and Paul T. Costa Jr., 'Personality trait structure as a human universal', *American Psychologist* 52, no. 5 (1997): 509.

3 Lewis R. Goldberg, 'An alternative "description of personality": The big-five factor structure', *Journal of Personality and Social Psychology* 59, no. 6 (1990): 1216.

4 Paul T. Costa Jr. and Robert R. McCrae, 'Four ways five factors are basic', *Personality and Individual Differences* 13, no. 6 (1992): 653–65.

5 Paul T. Costa and Robert R. McCrae, 'Normal personality assessment in clinical practice: The NEO Personality Inventory', *Psychological Assessment* 4, no. 1 (1992): 5.

6 Peter Borkenau and Anette Liebler, 'Observable attributes as manifestations and cues of personality and intelligence', *Journal of Personality* 63, no. 1 (1995): 1–25.

7 Robert R. McCrae and Paul T. Costa, *Personality in Adulthood: A Five-factor Theory Perspective* (New York City: Guilford Press, 2003).

8 Kelci Harris and Simine Vazire, 'On friendship development and the Big Five personality traits', *Social and Personality Psychology Compass* 10, no. 11 (2016): 647–67.

9 David C. Rowe, Mary Clapp and Janette Wallis, 'Physical attractiveness and the personality resemblance of identical twins', *Behavior Genetics* 17, no. 2 (1987): 191–201.

10 Kira-Anne Pelican, Robert Ward and Jamie Sherry, 'The Pleistocene protagonist: An evolutionary framework for the analysis of film protagonists', *Journal of Screenwriting* 7, no. 3 (2016): 331–49.

11 Sanjay Srivastava, Oliver P. John, Samuel D. Gosling and Jeff Potter, 'Development of personality in early and middle adulthood: Set like plaster or persistent change?' *Journal of Personality and Social Psychology* 84, no. 5 (2003): 1041.

12 Randy Stein and Alexander B. Swan, 'Evaluating the validity of Myers–Briggs type indicator theory: A teaching tool and window into intuitive psychology', *Social and Personality Psychology Compass* 13, no. 2 (2019): e12434.

13 William Fleeson, 'Toward a structure-and process-integrated view of personality: Traits as density distributions of states', *Journal of Personality and Social Psychology* 80, no. 6 (2001): 1011.

14 William Fleeson, Adriane B. Malanos and Noelle M. Achille, 'An intraindividual process approach to the relationship between extraversion and positive affect: Is acting extraverted as "good" as being extraverted?' *Journal of Personality and Social Psychology* 83, no. 6 (2002): 1409.

15 Kennon M. Sheldon, Richard M. Ryan, Laird J. Rawsthorne and Barbara Ilardi, 'Trait self and true self: Cross-role variation in the Big-Five personality traits and its relations with psychological authenticity and subjective well-being', *Journal of Personality and Social Psychology* 73, no. 6 (1997): 1380.

16 Paul T. Costa Jr., Antonio Terracciano and Robert R. McCrae, 'Gender differences in personality traits across cultures: Robust and surprising findings', *Journal of Personality and Social Psychology* 81, no. 2 (2001): 322.

17 Pim Cuijpers, Filip Smit, Brenda W. J. H. Penninx, Ron de Graaf, Margreet ten Have and Aartjan T. F. Beekman, 'Economic costs of neuroticism: A population-based study', *Archives of General Psychiatry* 67, no. 10 (2010): 1086–93.

18 Tim Bogg and Brent W. Roberts, 'Conscientiousness and health-related behaviors: A meta-analysis of the leading behavioral contributors to mortality', *Psychological Bulletin* 130, no. 6 (2004): 887.

19 Roman Kotov, Wakiza Gamez, Frank Schmidt and David Watson, 'Linking "big" personality traits to anxiety, depressive, and substance use disorders: A meta-analysis', *Psychological Bulletin* 136, no. 5 (2010): 768.

20 Donald R. Lynam and Joshua D. Miller, 'The basic trait of Antagonism: An unfortunately underappreciated construct', *Journal of Research in Personality* 81 (2019): 118–26.

21 Delroy L. Paulhus and Kevin M. Williams, 'The dark triad of personality: Narcissism, Machiavellianism, and psychopathy', *Journal of Research in Personality* 36, no. 6 (2002): 556–63.

Chapter 3

1 François Mairesse and Marilyn Walker, 'Automatic recognition of personality in conversation', in *Proceedings of the Human Language Technology Conference of the NAACL, Companion Volume: Short Papers* (Association for Computational Linguistics, 2006), 85–8.

2 Alastair J. Gill and Jon Oberlander, 'Taking care of the linguistic features of extraversion', *Proceedings of the Annual Meeting of the Cognitive Science Society* 24, no. 24 (2002).

3 James W. Pennebaker and Laura A. King, 'Linguistic styles: Language use as an individual difference', *Journal of Personality and Social Psychology* 77, no. 6 (1999): 1296.

4 Pennebaker and King, 'Linguistic styles: Language use as an individual difference'.

5 François Mairesse, Marilyn A. Walker, Matthias R. Mehl and Roger K. Moore, 'Using linguistic cues for the automatic recognition of personality in conversation and text', *Journal of Artificial Intelligence Research* 30 (2007): 457–500.

6 Matthias R. Mehl, Samuel D. Gosling and James W. Pennebaker, 'Personality in its natural habitat: Manifestations and implicit folk theories of personality in daily life', *Journal of Personality and Social Psychology* 90, no. 5 (2006): 862.

7 Gill and Oberlander, 'Taking care of the linguistic features of extraversion'.

8 Mairesse and Walker, 'Automatic recognition of personality in conversation'.

9 Alastair Gill and Jon Oberlander, 'Looking forward to more extraversion with n-grams', *Determination of Information and Tenor in Texts: Multiple Approaches to Discourse* 2003 (2003): 125–37.

10 Jean-Marc Dewaele and Adrian Furnham, 'Extraversion: The unloved variable in applied linguistic research', *Language Learning* 49, no. 3 (1999): 509–44.

11 Mehl et al., 'Personality in its natural habitat: Manifestations and implicit folk theories of personality in daily life'.

12 Dewaele and Furnham, 'Extraversion: The unloved variable in applied linguistic research'.

13 Pennebaker and King, 'Linguistic styles: Language use as an individual difference'.

14 Mehl et al., 'Personality in its natural habitat: Manifestations and implicit folk theories of personality in daily life'.

15 Mairesse and Walker, 'Automatic recognition of personality in conversation'.

16 Christina U. Heinrich and Peter Borkenau, 'Deception and deception detection: The role of cross-modal inconsistency', *Journal of Personality* 66, no. 5 (1998): 687–712.

17 Mairesse and Walker, 'Automatic recognition of personality in conversation'.

18 Mairesse and Walker, 'Automatic recognition of personality in conversation'.

19 Pennebaker and King, 'Linguistic styles: Language use as an individual difference'.

20 Mairesse et al., 'Using linguistic cues for the automatic recognition of personality in conversation and text'.

21 Mairesse and Walker, 'Automatic recognition of personality in conversation'.

22 Mairesse et al., 'Using linguistic cues for the automatic recognition of personality in conversation and text'.

23 Mairesse et al., 'Using linguistic cues for the automatic recognition of personality in conversation and text'.

24 Pennebaker and King, 'Linguistic styles: Language use as an individual difference'.

25 Mairesse et al., 'Using linguistic cues for the automatic recognition of personality in conversation and text'.

26 Mehl et al., 'Personality in its natural habitat: Manifestations and implicit folk theories of personality in daily life'.

27 Matthew L. Newman, Carla J. Groom, Lori D. Handelman and James W. Pennebaker, 'Gender differences in language use: An analysis of 14,000 text samples', *Discourse Processes* 45, no. 3 (2008): 211–36.

28 James W. Pennebaker and Lori D. Stone, 'Words of wisdom: Language use over the life span', *Journal of Personality and Social Psychology* 85, no. 2 (2003): 291.

29 James W. Pennebaker, Cindy K. Chung, Joey Frazee, Gary M. Lavergne and David I. Beaver, 'When small words foretell academic success: The case of college admissions essays.' *PloS one* 9, no. 12 (2014): e115844.

30 James W. Pennebaker, Matthias R. Mehl and Kate G. Niederhoffer, 'Psychological aspects of natural language use: Our words, our selves', *Annual Review of Psychology* 54, no. 1 (2003): 547–77.

Chapter 4

1 Larry C. Bernard, Michael Mills, Leland Swenson and R. Patricia Walsh, 'An evolutionary theory of human motivation', *Genetic, Social, and General Psychology Monographs* 131, no. 2 (2005): 129–84.

2   Daniel Nettle, 'The wheel of fire and the mating game: Explaining the origins
    of tragedy and comedy', *Journal of Cultural and Evolutionary Psychology* 3, no. 1
    (2005): 39–56.
3   Bernard et al., 'An evolutionary theory of human motivation'.
4   Bernard et al., 'An evolutionary theory of human motivation'.
5   Bernard et al., 'An evolutionary theory of human motivation'.
6   Steven Arnocky, Tina Piché, Graham Albert, Danielle Ouellette and Pat Barclay,
    'Altruism predicts mating success in humans', *British Journal of Psychology* 108,
    no. 2 (2017): 416–35.
7   Bernard et al., 'An evolutionary theory of human motivation'.
8   Bernard et al., 'An evolutionary theory of human motivation'.
9   Syd Field, *Screenplay: The Foundations of Screenwriting* (London: Delta, 2005).
10 Richard M. Ryan and Edward L. Deci, 'Self-determination theory and the
    facilitation of intrinsic motivation, social development, and well-being', *American
    Psychologist* 55, no. 1 (2000): 68.
11 Alexandra M. Freund, Marie Hennecke and M. Mustafic, 'On gains and losses,
    means and ends: Goal orientation and goal focus across adulthood', in *The
    Oxford Handbook of Human Motivation*, ed. Richard M. Ryan (New York: Oxford
    University Press, 2012).
12 Edward L. Deci and Richard M. Ryan, 'Motivation, personality, and development
    within embedded social contexts: An overview of self-determination theory', *The
    Oxford Handbook of Human Motivation* (2012): 85–107.
13 Freund et al., 'On gains and losses, means and ends: Goal orientation and goal focus
    across adulthood'.
14 Raymond B. Miller and Stephanie J. Brickman, 'A model of future-oriented
    motivation and self-regulation', *Educational Psychology Review* 16, no. 1
    (2004): 9–33.
15 Alison P. Lenton, Martin Bruder, Letitia Slabu and Constantine Sedikides, 'How
    does "being real" feel? The experience of state authenticity', *Journal of Personality* 81,
    no. 3 (2013): 276–89.
16 Matthew Vess, 'Varieties of conscious experience and the subjective awareness of
    one's "true" self', *Review of General Psychology* 23, no. 1 (2019): 89–98.
17 Katrina P. Jongman-Sereno and Mark R. Leary, 'The enigma of being yourself:
    A critical examination of the concept of authenticity', *Review of General Psychology*,
    no. 7 (2018): 32–9.
18 Stefan Bracha, Andrew E. Williams and Adam S. Bracha, 'Does "fight-or-flight"
    need updating?' *Psychosomatics* 45, no. 5 (2004): 448–9.
19 Kasia Kozlowska, Peter Walker, Loyola McLean and Pascal Carrive, 'Fear and
    the defense cascade: Clinical implications and management', *Harvard Review of
    Psychiatry* 23, no. 4 (2015): 263.

20 Shelley E. Taylor, Laura Cousino Klein, Brian P. Lewis, Tara L. Gruenewald, Regan A. R. Gurung and John A. Updegraff, 'Biobehavioral responses to stress in females: Tend-and-befriend, not fight-or-flight', *Psychological Review* 107, no. 3 (2000): 411.

21 Henk Aarts, Kirsten I. Ruys, Harm Veling, Robert A. Renes, Jasper H. B. de Groot, Anna M. van Nunen and Sarit Geertjes, 'The art of anger: Reward context turns avoidance responses to anger-related objects into approach.' *Psychological Science* 21, no. 10 (2010): 1406–10.

22 Antonio R. Damasio, 'Emotions and feelings', in *Feelings and Emotions: The Amsterdam Symposium* (Cambridge, UK: Cambridge University Press, 2004), 49–57.

23 Erika A. Patall, 'The motivational complexity of choosing: A review of theory and research', *The Oxford Handbook of Human Motivation* (2012): 248.

Chapter 5

1 Ulrich Orth, Ruth Yasemin Erol and Eva C. Luciano, 'Development of self-esteem from age 4 to 94 years: A meta-analysis of longitudinal studies', *Psychological Bulletin* 144, no. 10 (2018): 1045.

2 Erik H. Erikson and Joan M. Erikson, *The Life Cycle Completed (Extended Version)* (London: W.W. Norton & Company, 1998).

3 Erikson and Erikson, *The Life Cycle Completed (Extended Version)*.

4 Dan P. McAdams and Bradley D. Olson, 'Personality development: Continuity and change over the life course', *Annual Review of Psychology* 61 (2010): 517–42.

5 Erikson and Erikson, *The Life Cycle Completed (Extended Version)*.

6 Orth et al., 'Development of self-esteem from age 4 to 94 years: A meta-analysis of longitudinal studies'.

7 Erikson and Erikson, *The Life Cycle Completed (Extended Version)*.

8 Dan P. McAdams, *The Redemptive Self: Stories Americans Live By – Revised and Expanded Edition* (Oxford: Oxford University Press, 2013).

9 Martin J. Sliwinski, David M. Almeida, Joshua Smyth and Robert S. Stawski, 'Intraindividual change and variability in daily stress processes: Findings from two measurement-burst diary studies', *Psychology and Aging* 24, no. 4 (2009): 828.

10 Beatriz Fabiola López Ulloa, Valerie Møller and Alfonso Sousa-Poza, 'How does subjective well-being evolve with age? A literature review', *Journal of Population Ageing* 6, no. 3 (2013): 227–46.

11 Elaine Wethington, 'Expecting stress: Americans and the "midlife crisis"', *Motivation and Emotion* 24, no. 2 (2000): 85–103.

12 McAdams and Olson, 'Personality development: Continuity and change over the life course'.

13 Orth et al., 'Development of self-esteem from age 4 to 94 years: A meta-analysis of longitudinal studies'.

14 David G. Blanchflower and Andrew J. Oswald, 'Is well-being U-shaped over the life cycle?' *Social Science & Medicine* 66, no. 8 (2008): 1733–49.

15 Dan P. McAdams, *Power, intimacy, and the life story: Personological inquiries into identity* (New York: Guilford press, 1988).

16 Abraham H. Maslow, *Toward a psychology of being* (New York: Simon and Schuster, 2013).

17 Gayle Privette and Charles M. Brundrick, 'Peak experience, peak performance, and flow: Correspondence of personal descriptions and theoretical constructs', *Journal of Social Behavior and Personality* 6, no. 5 (1991): 169.

18 Richard Whitehead and Glen Bates, 'The transformational processing of peak and nadir experiences and their relationship to eudaimonic and hedonic well-being', *Journal of Happiness Studies* 17, no. 4 (2016): 1577–98.

19 Whitehead and Bates, 'The transformational processing of peak and nadir experiences and their relationship to eudaimonic and hedonic well-being'.

20 Nina Sarubin, Martin Wolf, Ina Giegling, Sven Hilbert, Felix Naumann, Diana Gutt, Andrea Jobst et al. 'Neuroticism and extraversion as mediators between positive/negative life events and resilience.' *Personality and Individual Differences* 82 (2015): 193–8.

21 P. Alex Linley and Stephen Joseph, 'Positive change following trauma and adversity: A review', *Journal of Traumatic Stress: Official Publication of the International Society for Traumatic Stress Studies* 17, no. 1 (2004): 11–21.

22 Dan P. McAdams, 'Coding autobiographical episodes for themes of agency and communion', *Unpublished Manuscript, Northwestern University, Evanston, IL* 212 (2001).

23 McAdams, Dan P. and Philip. J. Bowman. 'Narrating life's turning points: Redemption and contamination', in *Turns in the Road: Narrative Studies of Lives in Transition*, ed. Dan P. McAdams, Ruthellen H. Josselson and Amia Lieblich (Washington, DC: American Psychological Association, 2001), 3–34.

24 Jeffrey R. Measelle, Oliver P. John, Jennifer C. Ablow, Philip A. Cowan and Carolyn P. Cowan, 'Can children provide coherent, stable, and valid self-reports on the big five dimensions? A longitudinal study from ages 5 to 7', *Journal of Personality and Social Psychology* 89, no. 1 (2005): 90.

25 Jule Specht, Boris Egloff and Stefan C. Schmukle, 'Stability and change of personality across the life course: The impact of age and major life events on mean-level and rank-order stability of the Big Five', *Journal of Personality and Social Psychology* 101, no. 4 (2011): 862.

26 Paul T. Costa Jr. and Robert R. McCrae, 'Age changes in personality and their origins: Comment on Roberts, Walton, and Viechtbauer. *Psychological Bulletin 132*, no. 1 (2006): 26–8.

27 McAdams, *The Redemptive Self: Stories Americans Live By - Revised and Expanded Edition.*

28 Paul Bloom and Karen Wynn, 'What develops in moral development', in *Core Knowledge and Conceptual Change*, ed. David Barner and Andrew Scott Baron (Oxford: Oxford University Press, 2016), 347–64. John R. Snarey, 'Cross-cultural universality of social-moral development: A critical review of Kohlbergian research.' *Psychological Bulletin* 97, no. 2 (1985): 202.

29 M. Kent Jennings, Laura Stoker and Jake Bowers, 'Politics across generations: Family transmission reexamined', *The Journal of Politics* 71, no. 3 (2009): 782–99.

30 Dean R. Hoge, Gregory H. Petrillo and Ella I. Smith, 'Transmission of religious and social values from parents to teenage children', *Journal of Marriage and the Family* 44, no.3 (1982): 569–80.

31 Alain Van Hiel and Ivan Mervielde, 'Openness to experience and boundaries in the mind: Relationships with cultural and economic conservative beliefs', *Journal of Personality* 72, no. 4 (2004): 659–86.

32 Leon Festinger, *A Theory of Cognitive Dissonance*, vol. 2 (Stanford, CA: Stanford University Press, 1962).

33 Claude M. Steele, 'The psychology of self-affirmation: Sustaining the integrity of the self', in *Advances in Experimental Social Psychology*, vol. 21 (Academic Press, 1988), 261–302.

34 Herbert C. Kelman, 'Compliance, identification, and internalization: Three processes of attitude change.' *Journal of Conflict Resolution* 2, no. 1 (1958): 51–60.

35 Kelman, 'Compliance, identification, and internalization: Three processes of attitude change.'

36 Gregory R. Maio, Geoffrey Haddock and Bas Verplanken, *The Psychology of Attitudes and Attitude Change* (Los Angeles, CA: Sage Publications Limited, 2018).

Chapter 6

1 Elaine Hatfield, John T. Cacioppo and Richard L. Rapson, 'Emotional contagion', *Current Directions in Psychological Science* 2, no. 3 (1993): 96–100.

2 Soukayna Bekkali, George Youssef, Peter H. Donaldson, Natalia Albein-Urios, Christian Hyde and Peter Gregory Enticott, 'Is the Putative Mirror Neuron System Associated with Empathy? A Systematic Review and Meta-Analysis' (2019). PsyArXiv. March 20. doi:10.31234/osf.io/6bu4p.

3 Dolf Zillman and Joanne R. Cantor, 'Affective responses to the emotions of a protagonist', *Journal of Experimental Social Psychology* 13, no. 2 (1977): 155–65.

4 Robert L. Trivers, 'The evolution of reciprocal altruism', *The Quarterly Review of Biology* 46, no. 1 (1971): 35–57.

5 Mina Tsay and K. Maja Krakowiak, 'The impact of perceived character similarity and identification on moral disengagement', *International Journal of Arts and Technology* 4, no. 1 (2011): 102–10.

6 Arthur A. Raney, 'Expanding disposition theory: Reconsidering character liking, moral evaluations, and enjoyment', *Communication Theory* 14, no. 4 (2004): 348–69.

7 Paul Ekman, Wallace V. Friesen, Maureen O'Sullivan, Anthony Chan, Irene Diacoyanni-Tarlatzis, Karl Heider, Rainer Krause et al. 'Universals and cultural differences in the judgments of facial expressions of emotion', *Journal of Personality and Social Psychology* 53, no. 4 (1987): 712.

8 Nancy Rumbaugh Whitesell and Susan Harter, 'The interpersonal context of emotion: Anger with close friends and classmates', *Child Development* 67, no. 4 (1996): 1345–59.

9 Jesus Sanz, María Paz García-Vera and Ines Magan, 'Anger and hostility from the perspective of the Big Five personality model', *Scandinavian Journal of Psychology* 51, no. 3 (2010): 262–70.

10 Lauri A. Jensen-Campbell, Jennifer M. Knack, Amy M. Waldrip and Shaun D. Campbell. 'Do Big Five personality traits associated with self-control influence the regulation of anger and aggression?' *Journal of Research in Personality* 41, no. 2 (2007): 403–24.

11 Louise Helen Phillips, Julie D. Henry, Judith A. Hosie and Alan B. Milne, 'Age, anger regulation and well-being', *Aging and Mental Health* 10, no. 3 (2006): 250–6.

12 Christine Ma-Kellams and Jennifer Lerner, 'Trust your gut or think carefully? Examining whether an intuitive, versus a systematic, mode of thought produces greater empathic accuracy', *Journal of Personality and Social Psychology* 111, no. 5 (2016): 674.

13 Ken-Ichi Ohbuchi, Toru Tamura, Brian M. Quigley, James T. Tedeschi, Nawaf Madi, Michael H. Bond and Amelie Mummendey, 'Anger, blame, and dimensions of perceived norm violations: Culture, gender, and relationships', *Journal of Applied Social Psychology* 34, no. 8 (2004): 1587–603.

14 Steven Pinker, 'Toward a consilient study of literature', *Philosophy and Literature* 31, no. 1 (2007): 162–78.

15 Olivier Morin, Alberto Acerbi and Oleg Sobchuk, 'Why people die in novels: Testing the ordeal simulation hypothesis', *Palgrave Communications* 5, no. 1 (2019): 2.

16 Megan Oaten, Richard J. Stevenson and Trevor I. Case, 'Disgust as a disease-avoidance mechanism', *Psychological Bulletin* 135, no. 2 (2009): 303.

17 Carlos David Navarrete and Daniel M. T. Fessler, 'Disease avoidance and ethnocentrism: The effects of disease vulnerability and disgust sensitivity on intergroup attitudes', *Evolution and Human Behavior* 27, no. 4 (2006): 270–82.

18 Jonathan Haidt, Paul Rozin, Clark McCauley and Sumio Imada, 'Body, psyche, and culture: The relationship between disgust and morality', *Psychology and Developing Societies* 9, no. 1 (1997): 107–31.

19 Barbara L. Fredrickson, 'The role of positive emotions in positive psychology: The broaden-and-build theory of positive emotions', *American Psychologist* 56, no. 3 (2001): 218.

20 Julian Hanich, Valentin Wagner, Mira Shah, Thomas Jacobsen and Winfried Menninghaus, 'Why we like to watch sad films: The pleasure of being moved in aesthetic experiences', *Psychology of Aesthetics, Creativity, and the Arts* 8, no. 2 (2014): 130.

21 Mary Beth Oliver and Tilo Hartmann, 'Exploring the role of meaningful experiences in users' appreciation of "good movies"', *Projections* 4, no. 2 (2010): 128–50.

22 Sandro Mendonça, Gustavo Cardoso and João Caraça, 'The strategic strength of weak signal analysis', *Futures* 44, no. 3 (2012): 218–28.

23 Jonathan Haidt, 'Elevation and the positive psychology of morality', *Flourishing: Positive Psychology and the Life Well-Lived* 275 (2003): 289.

24 Dacher Keltner and Jonathan Haidt, 'Approaching awe, a moral, spiritual, and aesthetic emotion', *Cognition and Emotion* 17, no. 2 (2003): 297–314.

25 Amie M. Gordon, Jennifer E. Stellar, Craig L. Anderson, Galen D. McNeil, Daniel Loew and Dacher Keltner, 'The dark side of the sublime: Distinguishing a threat-based variant of awe', *Journal of Personality and Social Psychology* 113, no. 2 (2017): 310.

26 Moritz Lehne and Stefan Koelsch, 'Toward a general psychological model of tension and suspense.' *Frontiers in Psychology* 6 (2015): 79.

27 Lehne and Koelsch, 'Toward a general psychological model of tension and suspense'.

28 Lehne and Koelsch, 'Toward a general psychological model of tension and suspense'.

29 Brian Lickel, Toni Schmader, Mathew Curtis, Marchelle Scarnier and Daniel R. Ames, 'Vicarious shame and guilt.' *Group Processes & Intergroup Relations* 8, no. 2 (2005): 145–57.

30 Lickel et al., 'Vicarious shame and guilt'.

31 Robin L. Nabi, 'Emotional flow in persuasive health messages', *Health Communication* 30, no. 2 (2015): 114–24.

32 Kurt Vonnegut, *Palm Sunday: An Autobiographical Collage* (New York City: Dial Press, 1999).

33 Matthew L. Jockers, Interview with author. Zoom call. June 27, 2019.

34 Andrew J. Reagan, Lewis Mitchell, Dilan Kiley, Christopher M. Danforth and Peter Sheridan Dodds, 'The emotional arcs of stories are dominated by six basic shapes', *EPJ Data Science* 5, no. 1 (2016): 31.

35 Jodie Archer and Matthew L. Jockers, *The Bestseller Code: Anatomy of the Blockbuster Novel* (London: Penguin Random House, 2017).

36 Marco Del Vecchio, Alexander Kharlamov, Glenn Parry and Ganna Pogrebna, 'The data science of Hollywood: Using emotional arcs of movies to drive business model innovation in entertainment industries' (30 May 2018). Available at SSRN: https://ssrn.com/abstract=3198315 or http://dx.doi.org/10.2139/ssrn.3198315

37 Del Vecchio et al., 'The data science of Hollywood: Using emotional arcs of movies to drive business model innovation in entertainment industries".

38 Archer and Jockers, *The Bestseller Code: Anatomy of the Blockbuster Novel*.

39 Del Vecchio et al., 'The data science of Hollywood: Using emotional arcs of movies to drive business model innovation in entertainment industries'.

40 Del Vecchio et al., 'The data science of Hollywood: Using emotional arcs of movies to drive business model innovation in entertainment industries'.

41 Archer and Jockers, *The Bestseller Code: Anatomy of the Blockbuster Novel*.

42 Archer and Jockers, *The Bestseller Code: Anatomy of the Blockbuster novel*.

43 Del Vecchio et al., 'The data science of Hollywood: Using emotional arcs of movies to drive business model innovation in entertainment industries'.

44 Archer and Jockers, *The Bestseller Code: Anatomy of the Blockbuster Novel*.

45 Del Vecchio et al., 'The data science of Hollywood: Using emotional arcs of movies to drive business model innovation in entertainment industries'.

46 Archer and Jockers, *The Bestseller Code: Anatomy of the Blockbuster Novel*.

47 Shelley E. Taylor and David A. Armor, 'Positive illusions and coping with adversity', *Journal of Personality* 64, no. 4 (1996): 873–98.

48 Tali Sharot, 'The optimism bias', *Current Biology* 21, no. 23 (2011): R941–5.

49 Ajit Varki, 'Human uniqueness and the denial of death', *Nature* 460, no. 7256 (2009): 684.

50 McAdams, *The Redemptive Self: Stories Americans Live By – Revised and Expanded Edition*.

51 M. B. Oliver and A. A. Raney, 'Entertainment as pleasurable and meaningful: Identifying hedonic and eudaimonic motivations for entertainment consumption', *Journal of Communication* 61, no. 5 (2011): 984–1004.

52 Oliver and Raney, 'Entertainment as pleasurable and meaningful: Identifying hedonic and eudaimonic motivations for entertainment consumption'.

53 Hal Ersner-Hershfield, Joseph A. Mikels, Sarah J. Sullivan and Laura L. Carstensen, 'Poignancy: Mixed emotional experience in the face of meaningful endings', *Journal of Personality and Social Psychology* 94, no. 1 (2008): 158.

Chapter 7

1 Dana R. Carney, C. Randall Colvin and Judith A. Hall, 'A thin slice perspective on the accuracy of first impressions', *Journal of Research in Personality* 41, no. 5 (2007): 1054–72.
2 Alex L. Jones, Robin S. S. Kramer and Robert Ward, 'Signals of personality and health: The contributions of facial shape, skin texture, and viewing angle', *Journal of Experimental Psychology: Human Perception and Performance* 38, no. 6 (2012): 1353.
3 Jerry S. Wiggins and Ross Broughton, 'The interpersonal circle: A structural model for the integration of personality research', *Perspectives in Personality* 1 (1985): 1–47.
4 Maarten Selfhout, William Burk, Susan Branje, Jaap Denissen, Marcel Van Aken and Wim Meeus, 'Emerging late adolescent friendship networks and Big Five personality traits: A social network approach', *Journal of Personality* 78, no. 2 (2010): 509–38.
5 Kelci Harris and Simine Vazire, 'On friendship development and the Big Five personality traits', *Social and Personality Psychology Compass* 10, no. 11 (2016): 647–67.
6 Jochen E. Gebauer, Mark R. Leary and Wiebke Neberich, 'Big Two personality and Big Three mate preferences: Similarity attracts, but country-level mate preferences crucially matter.' *Personality and Social Psychology Bulletin* 38, no. 12 (2012): 1579–93.
7 Gebauer et al., 'Big Two personality and Big Three mate preferences: Similarity attracts, but country-level mate preferences crucially matter'.
8 Beatrice Rammstedt and Jürgen Schupp, 'Only the congruent survive – Personality similarities in couples', *Personality and Individual Differences* 45, no. 6 (2008): 533–5.
9 Michelle N. Shiota and Robert W. Levenson, 'Birds of a feather don't always fly farthest: Similarity in Big Five personality predicts more negative marital satisfaction trajectories in long-term marriages', *Psychology and Aging* 22, no. 4 (2007): 666.

10 D. Christopher Dryer and Leonard M. Horowitz, 'When do opposites attract? Interpersonal complementarity versus similarity', *Journal of Personality and Social Psychology* 72, no. 3 (1997): 592.

11 Kerry L. Jang, W. John Livesley and Philip A. Vemon, 'Heritability of the big five personality dimensions and their facets: A twin study', *Journal of Personality* 64, no. 3 (1996): 577–92.

12 Tena Vukasović and Denis Bratko, 'Heritability of personality: A meta-analysis of behavior genetic studies,' *Psychological Bulletin* 141, no. 4 (2015): 769.

13 David M. Buss, 'Manipulation in close relationships: Five personality factors in interactional context.' *Journal of Personality* 60, no. 2 (1992): 477–99.

14 Kipling D. Williams, 'Ostracism', *Annual Review of Psychology* 58 (2007).

15 Buss, 'Manipulation in close relationships: Five personality factors in interactional context.'

Chapter 8

1 Jones et al., 'Signals of personality and health: The contributions of facial shape, skin texture, and viewing angle.'

2 Carney et al., 'A thin slice perspective on the accuracy of first impressions.'

3 Jones et al., 'Signals of personality and health: The contributions of facial shape, skin texture, and viewing angle.'

Glossary

adaptive behaviour Behaviour which allows one to adapt effectively to one's environment.

agency An individual's desire to master their environment, assert the self, achieve power and competence.

agreeableness The disposition towards acting in a cooperative and unselfish manner. One of the Big Five personality dimensions.

altruism Seemingly unselfish behaviour which helps another at a cost to the individual.

backchannelling (in speech) A brief vocal expression that doesn't convey any important information but that shows the listener is continuing to pay attention to the speaker, for example, *uh-huh* or *right*.

closed to experience The disposition towards being closed to new cultural, aesthetic or intellectual experiences.

coercion The process of attempting to manipulate someone through the use of threats, force or other forms of negative power.

(cognitive) dissonance The unpleasant psychological state brought about by holding two opposing views or any other inconsistency within the mind.

communal An individual's desire to relate to, cooperate with and merge with others.

compliant The tendency to act in a submissive way.

conscientiousness The disposition towards acting in an organized, responsible, dutiful and hard-working way. One of the Big Five personality dimensions.

counter-dispositional Going against a cognitive, emotional or behavioural tendency.

debasement (or self-abasement) The act of putting oneself down or acting in a humiliating way.

disagreeableness The disposition towards behaving in a selfish and uncooperative manner.

disfluencies (in speech) Vocal interruptions in the regular flow of speech, for example, *uh* or *um*, pausing silently, repeating words, or interrupting oneself to correct something said previously.

distal goal A long-term goal that is accomplished over a longer period of time.

elevation (or moral elevation) The warm emotion elicited by witnessing virtuous acts of moral goodness.

emotional arc The emotional journey of a fictional character through the course of the narrative.

emotional contagion The rapid spread of emotion from one person (or character) to another.

emotional range The range of emotions that a fictional character experiences throughout the narrative.

emotional stability The disposition towards having stable moods and acting in a predictable and consistent manner.

extrinsic motivation Motivation that arises from the expectation of receiving an external reward.

extroversion (also extraversion) The disposition towards directing one's interests and energies towards the outward world. One of the Big Five personality dimensions.

facet (of personality) A specific aspect of a broader personality trait.

fight-or-flight response A pattern of physiological changes elicited as a result of a threatening or stressful situation that mobilizes energy towards either attacking or avoiding the threat.

generativity Fulfilling one's social obligations towards the next generation.

humanism Valuing the dignity and worth of every human.

intrinsic motivation Motivation that arises from taking pleasure in the activity itself rather than through anticipation of an external reward.

introversion The disposition towards directing one's interests and energies towards the internal private world.

Kantianism Treating people as ends unto themselves and not as a means towards achieving something else.

low point A difficult period during one's life in which they experience negative emotions including sadness, loss or grief.

Machiavellianism The personality trait defined by being calculating and treating others as a means to an end.

mirror neurons Brain cells that respond in the same way to an action whether the person performs the action themselves or sees someone else performing the action.

mixed affect (or mixed emotions) The simultaneous experience of both positive and negative feelings.

moral disengagement The process of convincing oneself that ethical standards do not apply in a particular situation.

moral emotions Social emotions that are linked to the welfare of society and are involved in moral judgements, for example, pride and disgust.

narcissism Excessive self-love or interest in oneself.

negative emotions Unpleasant or disruptive emotions that include sadness, anger, envy and fear.

neural reward circuits A group of neural structures that are associated with the desire to receive a reward, which usually leads to a positive emotional experience.

neuroticism The disposition towards emotional instability. One of the Big Five personality dimensions.

neutral emotions Neutral feelings without a positive or negative valence.

openness to experience The disposition towards being open to new intellectual, cultural or aesthetic experiences. One of the Big Five personality dimensions.

peak experience An emotional high point during someone's life, characterized by positive feelings of joy and transcendence.

positive emotions Uplifting emotions including contentment, happiness, joy, amusement, awe and love.

post-traumatic growth Positive psychological change after experiencing adversity or a traumatic event.

proximal goal A short-term goal that is achieved over a short period of time.

psychopathy (or antisocial personality disorder) The disposition towards disregarding and violating other people's rights.

PTSD (post-traumatic stress disorder) A chronic disorder, characterized by flashbacks, avoidance and physiological arousal, that may result from experiencing a particularly traumatic event.

reciprocal altruism The act of helping someone who later returns the favour.

regression Returning to a lower state of cognitive, behavioural or emotional functioning.

sentiment analysis The use of natural language processing and computational linguistics to analyze emotional states, for example, within text.

tender-mindedness The personality facet that measures the degree to which an individual's attitudes and judgements are influenced by their emotions.

turning point The critical moment at which someone has a major insight or makes the decision to change.

unconscientiousness The disposition towards acting in an unorganized and irresponsible way.

universal emotions Emotions that are universally experienced in very similar ways by all cultures.

Index